THE CASE FOR
Faith

• STUDENT EDITION •

Resources by Lee Strobel

The Unexpected Adventure (with Mark Mittelberg)

The Case for the Real Jesus

Finding the Real Jesus

The Case for Christ

The Case for Christ (audio)

The Case for Christ — Student Edition (with Jane Vogel)

The Case for Christ for Kids (with Rob Suggs)

The Case for Christmas

The Case for Christmas (audio)

The Case for a Creator

The Case for a Creator (audio)

The Case for a Creator — Student Edition (with Jane Vogel)

The Case for a Creator for Kids (with Rob Suggs)

The Case for Easter

The Case for Faith

The Case for Faith (audio)

The Case for Faith — Student Edition (with Jane Vogel)

The Case for Faith for Kids (with Rob Suggs)

Discussing the Da Vinci Code (curriculum; with Garry Poole)

Discussing the Da Vinci Code (discussion guide; with Garry Poole)

Exploring the Da Vinci Code (with Garry Poole)

Experiencing the Passion of Jesus (with Garry Poole)

Faith Under Fire (curriculum series)

God's Outrageous Claims

Inside the Mind of Unchurched Harry and Mary

Off My Case for Kids (with Robert Elmer)

Surviving a Spiritual Mismatch in Marriage (with Leslie Strobel)

Surviving a Spiritual Mismatch in Marriage (audio)

What Jesus Would Say

THE CASE FOR
Faith
• STUDENT EDITION •

A Journalist Investigates the
Toughest Objections to Christianity

New York Times Bestselling Author

LEE
STROBEL

with Jane Vogel

ZONDERVAN

The Case for Faith—Student Edition
Copyright © 2001 by Lee Strobel

This title is also available as a Zondervan ebook. Visit www.zondervan.com/ebooks.

Requests for information should be addressed to:
Zondervan, *Grand Rapids, Michigan 49530*

This edition: ISBN 978-0-310-74542-6

Library of Congress Cataloging-in-Publication Data

Strobel, Lee, 1952-
    The case for faith : a journalist investigates the toughest questions to Christian-
ity / by Lee Strobel, with Jane Vogel. — [New] student ed.
        p. cm.
    Includes bibliographical references.
    ISBN 978-0-310-24188-1
    1. Apologetics.   I. Vogel, Jane.   II. Title.
BT1102.577 2002
239.21   2001006890

Cover design: *Deborah Washburn*
Interior design: *Todd Sprague*

Printed in the United States of America

HB 07.27.2021

CONTENTS

Introduction: Questions Worth Asking　　　　　7

Objection #1:
Since Evil and Suffering Exist, a Good God Cannot　　11

Objection #2:
Miracles Contradict Science;　　29
Therefore They Cannot Be Real

Objection #3:
Evolution Explains Life, So God Isn't Needed　　41

Objection #4:
It's Intolerant to Claim Jesus Is the Only Way to God　　51

Objection #5:
A Loving God Would Never Send People to Hell　　63

Objection #6:
I Still Have Doubts, So I Can't Be a Christian　　73

Conclusion: The Power of Faith　　87

Questions Worth Asking

A re you ready? Let's roll!"

Those are the last words the GTE Airfone operator heard Todd Beamer say. After that, screams, the sounds of a scuffle, and then—silence. Fifteen minutes later, United Airlines Flight 93 crashed into the Pennsylvania countryside, taking Todd and the rest of the passengers and crew with it.

The fact that the plane crashed 80 miles southeast of Pittsburgh instead of into its intended target somewhere in Washington, D.C., is probably due in part to Todd's courage. Hijacked planes had already crashed into the World Trade Center and the Pentagon. Flight 93 was to have been the fourth plane used as a terrorist weapon that day.

By the time Todd made his Airfone call, the hijackers aboard Flight 93 had stabbed one passenger to death and injured both pilots. They had herded the remaining passengers into two groups, one in the front of the plane and one in the rear.

"We're going to do something," Todd told the operator, explaining his plans to jump on the hijacker guarding them. Todd believed the hijacker had a bomb strapped to his waist. "I know I'm not going to get out of this," he said.

Then he asked her to say the Lord's Prayer with him and to tell his two children and his wife, Lisa, who was expecting their third child, that he loved them.

FAITH ON FLIGHT 93

"If he gave up his life to save others, that would be Todd," Lisa said later.

What gives a man that kind of courage?

"Todd was a committed Christian, secure in his faith and his eternity," his wife wrote in a letter after the crash. Apparently that faith held strong to the very end. According to the Airfone operator, Todd's final words were, "God help me. Jesus help me. Are you ready? Let's roll!"

OBJECTIONS TO FAITH

"People live their lives and don't leave a legacy of faith and hope and love that Todd has left," Lisa Beamer told reporters after her husband's death. Many would like to be known as people of courage like Todd. But Todd was also a person of faith. And that's a different story. For some people—including me—that kind of faith can be hard to come by.

In fact, for much of my youth and adult life, I considered myself an atheist. Admittedly, I hadn't analyzed the evidence for and against God before I concluded that he didn't exist. It simply seemed to me that thinking people just weren't the religious type.

Why would I waste my time checking out the Christian faith? God and miracles—come on! It didn't take much of a dose of modern science to debunk that kind of Sunday school fantasy.

Then the unthinkable happened. My wife, Leslie, became a Christian. At first I was horrified. Then I was intrigued by the changes I started seeing in her life. Eventually I decided to check out the Christian faith. I would separate the make-believe from the reality and see what was left. After all, that's what I did every day as a journalist—I was experienced at investigating things to see what was true.

Why not put faith to the same test yourself?

UNSETTLING QUESTIONS

My previous book, *The Case for Christ*, described my nearly two-year investigation of the evidence that pointed me to the verdict that God really exists and that Jesus actually is his unique Son.

But even though I had become convinced of that, I still had some nagging objections. The last thing I wanted was a faith built on wishful thinking; I needed a faith grounded in reality. *Yes*, I could see how the evidence points to Jesus, *but* what about problems like these:

- If there's a loving God, why is there so much pain and suffering in the world?
- If miracles contradict science, how can any rational person believe they're true?
- If God really created the universe, then why does science point to evolution as the origin of life?
- If Jesus is the only way to heaven, then what about the millions of people who have never heard of him?
- If God cares about the people he created, how could he send many of them to hell?
- If I still have doubts, is it possible to be a Christian?

These are some of the most common questions people ask about God. In fact, these obstacles once stood solidly between me and faith. So I decided to retrace and expand on my spiritual journey. I wanted to explore once again whether there are satisfying answers to the hard questions that send nagging doubts into our hearts and minds. Can faith really stand up to reason? Is it possible to be a thinker and a Christian at the same time?

I committed myself to asking hard questions and not being satisfied with easy answers. I wanted to find out what both doubters and believers had to say about some of the most challenging obstacles to faith. Most of all, I wanted to find out whether God was telling the truth when he said, "When you look for me with all your heart, you will find me" (Jeremiah 29:13 NIrV).

If you've ever asked questions about faith, this book is for you. Come along as I retrace my journey, and I hope you'll find answers for yourself.

Are you ready? Let's roll.

Since Evil and Suffering Exist, a Good God Cannot

n Monday, September 10, 2001, the top story on the Chicago nightly news was the possibility that Michael Jordan might make a comeback. Every local station opened the newscast with the report that MJ had been working out and had promised to hold a press conference later in the week. Watching the news, you would have thought the only issue worth worrying about was whether Bulls fans could handle it if MJ came back to the game wearing a Wizards uniform.

On Tuesday, September 11, 2001, no one was thinking about basketball.

Because on Tuesday, September 11, terrorists hijacked two airliners and crashed the planes—with their civilian passengers—into the World Trade Towers in New York City. Another hijacked plane struck the Pentagon, while a fourth was prevented from hitting its intended target and went down outside Pittsburgh.

11

Thousands of Americans watched, horrified, as live TV coverage showed people leaping out of seventieth-story windows of the World Trade Towers to escape the searing flames inside. One man and woman were holding hands.

At 9:50 A.M., one tower collapsed straight down and vanished in a cloud of smoke and dust. It looked like something out of the movie *Independence Day.* The second tower collapsed forty minutes later. Dust and soot piled up in the streets around the trade center—burying bodies of the dead and dying. According to one Emergency Medical Service worker, "A lot of the vehicles are running over bodies because they are all over the place."

"Today, our nation saw evil," President George W. Bush said in an address to the nation that terrible Tuesday night.

WHERE IS GOD?

If there is a loving God in control of the world, how do you make sense out of the kind of evil and suffering that the world saw on September 11, 2001? Where is God when terrorist hijackers force their way into an airplane cockpit? Where is God when thousands of people are killed, and their families—including orphaned children—are left grieving?

If God is loving, all-powerful, and good, then it seems as if evil and suffering should not exist. After all, if God is all-powerful, then he should be able to prevent suffering. If he chooses not to, then how can he be considered good? For many people, that's one of the biggest objections to the Christian faith. Doesn't the very existence of such awful suffering prove that there is no such thing as a good, all-powerful God?

NO EASY ANSWERS

When I began my search for the answer to that question, the terrorist attacks hadn't yet occurred. But I had seen plenty of suffering as a journalist. What's more, my wife, Leslie, was facing the issue personally. Her uncle had just died, and her aunt had been diagnosed with both Alzheimer's disease and terminal cancer. Rocked by those experiences, Leslie was suspicious of anyone who might try to give easy answers.

"If someone thinks he can wrap everything up in a neat little package and put a fancy theological bow on it," she warned me, "go somewhere else."

I couldn't give you those answers in a neat little package even if I wanted to, because I don't have all the answers. I'm not sure anyone does. But what I can do is tell you the story of my struggle to make sense out of suffering. You can decide for yourself whether it makes sense to you.

IS IT GOD'S FAULT?

I decided to talk to a philosopher named Peter Kreeft about the problem of evil. I'd read some of Peter's books, and I knew he was smart and funny—and honest. I hoped he was also thick-skinned, because I planned to ask him some hard questions that might sound a little offensive to someone who believes in God.

I started at the beginning: "If there is a God, why didn't he make a world where people didn't hurt each other?"

Peter answered, "He did." At least, he added, that's what the Bible said things were like at the outset of human history.

(I have to say right here that I didn't always believe that the Bible was true. If that's the case for you, read the box "Can You Believe the Bible?")

"If God didn't create evil," I said, "then where did evil come from?"

"Once God chose to create human beings with free choice," Peter explained, "then it was up to them, rather than to God, whether there was evil or not. That's what free choice means. Built into the situation of God deciding to create human beings is the chance of evil and the suffering that results."

Can You Believe The Bible?

Talking about that question would take practically a whole book in itself. In fact, I do talk about whether you can believe the Bible in *The Case for Christ—Student Edition*, and even more in the longer edition of *The Case for Christ*. If you're interested, you can read it for yourself.

For now, let me just say that my experience—after a year and a half of exploring the question of the Bible's reliability—has led me to accept the Bible as trustworthy. If you're not sure about the Bible yourself, you can still explore what it says, in much the same way that a scientist works with a hypothesis even if the hypothesis hasn't been proven. You might find it helpful to ask yourself this question: *If* what the Bible says is true, do the conclusions I would draw from it make sense?

For instance, *if* the Bible is right about a God who created a world without human suffering, do the ideas about freedom of choice described in the section "Is It God's Fault?" make sense to you?

"Then why didn't God create human beings who were unable to choose to hate, or destroy, or to do all the other things that cause pain and suffering?" I pursued. "Why didn't he create people capable only of being kind and loving?"

"Think of it this way," Peter suggested. "If you push a button on one of those talking Barbie dolls, and it says, 'I love you,' how meaningful is that? If 'love' or 'goodness' is something programmed into you, something you have no choice about, is it really love? Real love must involve a choice."

Thinking about my own relationships, what Peter said made sense.

The Case for Faith

"God gave people free choice because that's the only way they could experience love, which is the greatest value in the universe," Peter continued, "but then humans abused their freedom of choice by rejecting God and walking away from him. And that's how human suffering came into the world."

As a philosopher, Peter had some things to say about "moral evil" and "natural evil"—you can read about that in the box "Droughts and Drive-bys" if you're interested. But I wanted to get back to the main issue.

"So by creating people with choices, God in effect *did* create evil," I persisted.

"God did *not* create evil and suffering," Peter said firmly. "Now, it's true that he *did* create the *potential* for evil to enter the world, because that was the only way to create the potential for authentic love. But it was human beings, with our free choice, who brought that potential into reality."

"But if God is God, couldn't he have known what would happen?" I asked. "Couldn't he have anticipated the consequences of giving people free choice?"

"No doubt he did," Peter agreed. "But let me ask *you* a question: When you start a new relationship—whether it's a friendship or a relationship that might possibly lead to falling in love—can you foresee the *possibility* that the other person may sometime disappoint you or hurt you or even walk away from you completely?"

I nodded.

"So why do you ever make friends or start relationships?" Peter asked.

"I guess it's because it's worth the risk," I said slowly. "Having good friends, and all the wonderful things about being in love with my wife—that more than makes up for the risk of getting hurt."

"I think it's the same with God," Peter said. "He knew we'd rebel against him, but he also knew many people would

Droughts and Drive-bys

It's pretty easy to see how human beings are responsible for a lot of the suffering in the world. Drive-by shootings, for instance. Philosophers call it "moral evil"—the immorality and suffering that come because people choose to be selfish, arrogant, uncaring, hateful, and abusive.

Some people estimate that 95% of the world's suffering results from human actions. For example, people look at a famine and wonder where God is, but the world produces enough food for each person to have 3,000 calories a day. It's human corruption and self-centeredness that keep people from being fed.

But what about the drought that caused the famine in the first place? Or other natural disasters, like earthquakes, floods, and tornadoes, that hurt people? Insurance companies sometimes call these "acts of God." Philosophers call them "natural evil"—bad stuff that humans experience but which can't be directly traced to some human action.

Or can they? Here's how Cliffe Knechtle explained it in his book *Give Me an Answer*: "When we humans told God to shove off, he partially honored our request. Nature began to revolt. Genetic breakdown and disease began. Pain and death become part of the human experience."[1]

We're realizing more and more how interconnected everything in the world really is. Cutting down rain forests leads to higher CO_2 levels, leading to a thinning of the ozone layer, leading to global warming, leading to increased melting of the polar ice caps, leading to increased flooding. . . . You get the idea. Is it so strange to think that human action and the natural world are connected in ways we may not see so clearly?

---

[1]Cliffe Knechtle, *Give Me an Answer* (Downers Grove, Ill.: InterVarsity Press, 1986), 52.

The Case for Faith

choose to follow him. It must be worth it to him, because he not only created us with free choice, but he even created the way to bring us back to him after we rebel—through the suffering of his Son Jesus."

WHY DOESN'T GOD WIPE OUT SUFFERING?

Peter had given me a lot to consider about where suffering comes from. But I wasn't about to let him—or God—off the hook yet.

"Even if God didn't cause suffering in the first place," I said, "why doesn't he put a stop to it now? If I sat and did nothing while my child got run over by a truck, I would be a bad father. When God sits by and refuses to perform miracles to keep people safe from even worse dangers than being hit by a truck, isn't he a bad God?"

"It looks like he is," Peter agreed. "But the fact that God deliberately allows certain things, which if we allowed them would turn us into monsters, doesn't necessarily count against God."

I couldn't see his reasoning. "You'll have to explain," I said.

"Okay," he replied. "If I said to my brother, 'I could bail you out of a problem but I won't,' I would probably be irresponsible and perhaps wicked. But we do that with children all the time. We don't do their homework for them. We don't put a bubble around them and protect them from every hurt.

"I remember when one of my daughters was trying to thread a needle in Brownies. It was very difficult for her. Every time she tried, she hit herself in the finger and a couple of times she bled. I was watching her but she didn't see me. My first instinct was to go and do it for her, but I said to myself, *She can do it.* After about five minutes she finally did it. I came out of hiding and she said, 'Daddy, Daddy—look what I did!'

She was so proud she had threaded the needle that she had forgotten all about the pain.

"That time pain was a good thing for her. I was wise enough to have foreseen it was good for her. Now, certainly God is much wiser than I was with my daughter. So it's at least possible that God is wise enough to foresee that we need some pain for reasons which we may not understand but which he foresees as being necessary to some eventual good. Therefore he's not being evil by allowing that pain to exist."

A Bear, a Hunter, and God

I could understand that if there was a God, his infinite wisdom would be much greater than our finite knowledge. But I needed more help in grasping how that affects suffering. When I mentioned this to Peter, he responded with a story.

"Imagine you're walking in the woods and come across a bear with his leg in a trap. You want to help him, but he thinks you're out to get him, so he fights you every time you get close. Finally, you shoot him with a tranquilizer gun. Now he really thinks you're out to hurt him!

"Then, to get his leg out of the trap, you first have to push it deeper into the trap to release the tension on the spring. If the bear were still semiconscious, he would be even more convinced you were out to hurt him. But he would be wrong! He can see the situation only from his limited perspective, so he wonders, *Why are you making me suffer?*"

Peter let the story sink in for a moment. "Now," he concluded, "how can you be sure it's not like that with us and God? I believe God does the same to us sometimes, and we can't understand why he does it any more than the bear could understand what you were doing. As the bear could have trusted you, so we can trust God."

USING SUFFERING

What if it's true that you can trust God the way that bear could trust me? How could God be using your pain and suffering to help you? I talked with a lot of people about their experiences with suffering, and some of the same themes kept coming up—themes they found echoed in what the Bible says about suffering.

Training

Ask champion athletes whether they simply floated to the top of their sport or whether instead their training involved teeth-gritting sacrifice and suffering. They'll tell you, "No pain, no gain." They probably wouldn't go so far as to say the pain was good in itself, but something good definitely resulted from it.

Just as a grueling workout helps an athlete build stamina and strength, difficult life experiences can shape a person's character to make him or her a winner in some other way. The Bible describes it like this: "We also rejoice in our sufferings, because we know that suffering produces perseverance; perseverance, character; and character, hope" (Romans 5:3).

I saw a real-life example of that in a guy in his mid-twenties named Craig. Craig really knows how to reach out to and help hurting teenagers. He mentioned that the best preparation he had for his work was going through his own broken engagement. Do you think that was suffering for him? If you've ever experienced a broken relationship, you know it was! Do you think he "rejoiced" in it? Not at the time, I'm sure! But can you imagine going through a breakup yourself and wanting someone to talk to about it? Who would you rather talk to: someone who has never felt that pain or someone who knows just what you're going through?

If you could ask Craig whether God can use painful experiences to strengthen him, what do you think he would say? (By the way, Craig just celebrated his second month of marriage to a woman who appreciates the strength Craig developed in that other, painful relationship.)

Midcourse Correction

Some people point to pain as an experience that redirects them. A woman I work with has a brother-in-law with Down's syndrome. For some reason, the connections that convey the message of pain through the nervous system don't work very well for him. He could rest his hand on the red-hot burner of an electric stove and not notice it until he was severely burned. If you or I did that, the pain we feel would make us snatch our hand back in a second. Physical pain protects you and me from something worse.

The Bible compares it to parental discipline: "Our fathers disciplined us for a little while as they thought best; but God disciplines us for our good, that we may share in his holiness. No discipline seems pleasant at the time, but painful. Later on, however, it produces a harvest of righteousness and peace for those who have been trained by it" (Hebrews 12:10–11).

That happened in a dramatic way in the life of a friend named Terry. He was going down the path of drug addiction and stealing, and it took the pain of a barroom brawl that knocked his teeth out, being robbed while he was stoned, and finally landing in prison to show him that crime and addiction are a dead-end road. In prison, he has committed himself to turning his life around.

I see it in less dramatic ways in my own life. Like the time I joined in on some thoughtless, unkind talk behind someone's back—and it turned out the person was right around the corner, hearing everything I said. I don't think I'll ever forget how miserable and embarrassed and sorry I felt—in fact, I hope I never do forget, because it was the kind of miserable feeling that made me realize I never wanted to do that again. The pain of that experience showed me some corrections I needed to make in my own behavior.

Let me emphasize, though, that the idea of God using pain to enable us to make midcourse corrections in our lives works better for understanding pain in my own life than for understanding pain in someone else's. If I tell someone, "God is letting you suffer because you've been going in the wrong direction," that's pretty much like saying, "It's your own fault you're suffering." When I hear people talking as if they can read God's mind about why a person is suffering, I cringe. There may be times when I need to call someone to that kind of accountability, but most of the time I think people need our support.

Positive from Negative

If you've talked with Christians about the question of suffering, you've probably heard these famous words from Romans 8:28: "And we know that in all things God works for the good of those who love him, who have been called according to his purpose." In other words, God will take bad circumstances and bring good out of them—if we're committed to following him.

That has even happened with the horror of the September 11 attacks. "None of us would ever wish the evil that has been

From Prisoner to Prime Minister

The classic example from the Bible of how God can bring good out of evil is the life of Joseph. His brothers sold him into slavery, his employer's wife framed him for a crime he didn't commit, his employer had him thrown in prison. Ultimately, though, Joseph rose to power and influence and was in a position to save the lives of his family and many others. (It's a great story; you can read it in Genesis 37–50.) Joseph summarized his life experience to his brothers this way: "You intended to harm me, but God intended it for good to accomplish what is now being done, the saving of many lives" (Genesis 50:20).

done to our country," said President Bush, "yet we have learned that out of evil can come great good.... We have seen it in the courage of passengers who rushed terrorists to save others on the ground. Passengers like an exceptional man named Todd Beamer.... We have seen the state of our Union in the endurance of rescuers working past exhaustion. We've seen the unfurling of flags, the lighting of candles, the giving of blood, the saying of prayers in English, Hebrew and Arabic.... Great harm has been done to us. We have suffered great loss. And in our grief and anger we have found our mission and our moment."

It's hard to deny that tragedy can bring out the best in people. But when Peter Kreeft suggested that God might allow some horrible things because more people will be better for it in the long run, I shook my head.

"That's still hard to accept," I told him. "It sounds like a cop-out to me."

"Okay, then let's put it to the test," Peter replied. "You see, God has shown us very clearly how this can work. He has demonstrated how the very worst thing that has ever happened in the history of the world ended up resulting in the very best thing that ever happened in the history of the world."

"What do you mean?"

"The death of God himself on the cross," he replied. "There Christ hung on the cross—forsaken by his friends and seemingly by God, bleeding to death and crying, 'My God, my God, why have you forsaken me?' And the result was that heaven was opened to human beings."

"But that was Jesus," I pointed out. "That's different."

"It's different because *your* death, or mine, wouldn't open heaven for anyone else," Peter agreed, "but maybe it's not so different in the way God works through suffering. When we face struggles and suffering, we sometimes can't imagine any good coming of it. But we've seen how it did in the case of

The Case for Faith

Jesus, and we can trust that it will in our case too. For instance, the greatest Christians in history seem to say that their sufferings ended up bringing them the closest to God—so this is the best thing that could happen, not the worst."

Getting Your Attention

"And that brings me to what may be the most important good thing that God could bring out of your pain and suffering," Peter said. "God might just use it to get your attention and draw you close to him."

In his book *The Problem of Pain*, writer C. S. Lewis says, "God whispers to us in our pleasures, speaks in our conscience, but shouts in our pains; it is his megaphone to rouse a deaf world."[2]

IT ISN'T FAIR

Even if God didn't create suffering, and even if God can use suffering to accomplish good things, I still had a complaint for Peter. "Evil people hurt others all the time. Surely God can't think that's fair! Terrorists and rapists and bullies on grade school playgrounds and the powerful people who make life miserable for their peers on high school campuses—why does God let them get away with it?"

"People *aren't* getting away with it," Peter insisted. "The fact that God *hasn't* evened the score in every case doesn't mean that he *won't*. Criticizing him for not doing it yet is like reading half a novel and then criticizing the author for not tying up the loose ends of the plot. In fact, the Bible says that the day will come when sickness and pain will be wiped out and people will be held accountable for the suffering they've caused."

"That might satisfy someone who is already convinced about God," I objected, "but what would you say to a skeptic

---

[2]C. S. Lewis, *The Problem of Pain* (New York: Macmillan, 1962), 93.

who asked, 'If God could end all this suffering right now, what's holding him up?'"

Peter chuckled. "I'd tell him, 'You are.'"

"Excuse me?"

Peter explained: "God promises that when he puts an end to suffering, the rewards for those who love him will more than make up for what they suffered. [See the box "Taking the Long View."] At the same time, he'll judge everyone who causes suffering. But he's delaying that day so that more people can put their trust in him and spend eternity with him. The Bible says, 'The Lord is not slow in keeping his promise, as some under-

The Megaphone of Pain

The number of prayer services that followed the attack on New York City seemed to suggest that Peter might be right. When things are going your way, how easy is it to forget about God? It's when things are going wrong that we turn to God—either for help or to blame him.

I don't know whether the prayer vigils following the World Trade Center tragedy represent a lasting faith or just a panicked reaching for God that will fade away when people feel their lives getting back to normal. But I know there are people who have gotten close to God through other kinds of suffering—and stayed close.

Maybe you know of Joni Eareckson Tada. Thirty years ago she was an active teenager with everything going for her—until she was paralyzed in a diving accident. Listen to her words about the pain that has drawn her to God: "I'd rather be in this wheelchair knowing God than on my feet without him." For Joni, if it took paralysis to bring her to God, she believes it was worth it.

stand slowness. He is patient with you, not wanting anyone to perish, but everyone to come to repentance' [2 Peter 3:9]. He's delaying everything out of love for me. For you."

When I look at it that way, my argument *against* the existence of a loving God looks more like evidence *for* a loving God—that he would care so much for me.

THE GOD WHO HOLDS OUR HANDS

My friend Marc Harrienger was with me when I did some of the research for this chapter. We were riding in his car together as I was trying to digest some of the things Peter Kreeft had said.

"It's true," Marc said, breaking the silence.

"What's true?" I asked.

"What Kreeft said—it's true. I know. I've lived it."

Several years earlier, Marc had been shoveling snow on his driveway when his wife said she was going to move the car and asked him to watch their young daughter. As the car backed out, they were suddenly thrust into the worst nightmare that parents can imagine: their toddler was crushed beneath a wheel.

Marc knows what it's like to hold a dying child in his arms.

At first his despair was so deep that he had to ask God to help him breathe, to help him eat, to help him function at the most fundamental level. Otherwise, he was paralyzed by the emotional pain. But he increasingly felt God's presence, his grace, his warmth, his comfort. Slowly, over time, Marc's wounds began to heal.

Marc experienced God at his point of greatest need, and he came through his grief a changed person. He gave up his career in business to attend seminary. Through his suffering— though he would never have chosen it, though it was horribly painful, though it was life-shattering at the time—Marc has been transformed into someone who will devote the rest of his life to bringing God's compassion to others who are alone in their desperation.

The first time he ever spoke in a church about Jesus, Marc was able to draw on his own experiences with God in the depths of sorrow. People were captivated because his own loss had given him special insights, empathy, and credibility. In the end, dozens of them responded by saying they too wanted to know this Jesus, this God of tears. Now other hearts are being healed because of Marc's having been broken. From one couple's despair comes new hope for many.

"Sometimes people roll their eyes at the Bible's saying that God can cause good to come from our pain if we run toward him instead of away from him," Marc said. "But I've watched it happen in my own life. I've experienced God's goodness through deep pain, and no one can dispute that. The God that some people deny is the same God who held our hands in the deep, dark places, who strengthened our marriage, who deepened our faith, who increased our reliance on him, who gave us two more children, and who infused our lives with new purpose and meaning so that we can make a difference to others."

I asked gently, "Do you wish you had more answers about why suffering happens in the first place?"

"We live in a broken world; Jesus was honest enough to tell us we'd have pain. Sure, I'd like to understand more about why. But the ultimate answer is Jesus' presence. That sounds sappy, I know. But just wait—when your world is rocked, you don't want philosophy or theology as much as you want the reality of Christ. He *was* the answer for me. He was the very answer we needed."

Miracles Contradict Science; Therefore They Cannot Be Real

ne time I saw Penn and Teller, the comedian-magicians, select a 10-year-old boy named Isaiah from the audience and show him a long strip of polyester, which they proceeded to knot and cut in the middle. Then, with a big flourish, they shook out the cloth and—voilà!—it was in one piece again.

"What do you think?" Penn asked Isaiah. "Was that a miracle or a magic trick?"

Isaiah didn't hesitate. "A magic trick," he replied with confidence.

Kids know enough about science to know that when we can't understand what might have caused a mysterious event, there's still probably a reasonable explanation apart from the miraculous.

But can a person be scientifically sophisticated and still believe in the possibility of miracles?

Many scientists see no conflict between science and their conclusion that a miracle-working

God is responsible for creating and sustaining the universe. (Check out the "Quotes to Consider" throughout this chapter.)

Is that a form of professional denial? Can a person write off elves and fairies as products of the imagination and yet at the same time accept manna from heaven, the virgin birth, and the Resurrection as being credible events of history? If miracles are direct violations of natural laws, then how can a reasonable person believe they could ever occur?

WHAT IF?

I remember a conversation I had with a philosopher named Bill Craig when I was exploring this whole question of miracles.

"Okay, Dr. Craig," I challenged him. "You're an intelligent and educated individual. Tell me: how can a modern and rational person still believe in babies being born from virgins, people walking on water, and cadavers emerging alive from tombs?"

Bill smiled. "It's funny you should ask specifically about the virgin birth," he replied, "because that was a major stumbling block to my becoming a Christian. I thought it was totally absurd."

"Really?" I said. "What happened?"

"When I was a teenager and I heard the Christian message for the first time, I had already studied biology. I know that for the virgin birth to be true, a Y chromosome had to be created out of nothing in Mary's ovum, because Mary didn't possess the genetic material to produce a male child. To me, this was utterly fantastic. It just didn't make sense."

"You're not alone," I agreed. "Other people have problems with that too. How did you go on from there?"

Bill thought back for a moment. "Well, I sort of put that issue aside and became a Christian anyway, even though I didn't really believe in the virgin birth. But then, after I became a Christian, it occurred to me that if I really do believe in a God who created the universe, then for him to create a Y chromosome would be child's play!"

"But I don't understand—how could you have become a Christian when you had doubts about a doctrine as significant as the virgin birth?"

"I guess the authenticity of the person of Jesus and the truth of his message were so powerful that they simply overwhelmed any other doubts I had," he replied.

I pressed him: "Weren't you rushing headlong into something you didn't totally accept?"

Quote To Consider

Miracles & the Laws of Nature
Do miracles contradict the natural laws of science?
Check out this quote.

Suppose an apple falls from a tree. That illustrates the law of gravity. The apple will simply fall to the ground. However, what if I reached out and caught the apple before it hit the ground? Am I overturning the law of gravity? Am I negating the law of gravity? No, not at all. All I'm doing is intervening.

And that's simply what God does when he performs a miracle. He doesn't suspend the natural laws that govern the world or overturn them; he simply chooses to intervene. If I can intervene to catch an apple before it hits the ground, then certainly God can intervene in a similar way to accomplish what he wants to accomplish.

J. P. MORELAND, PHILOSOPHER

"No, I don't think so," he said. "You don't need all your questions answered to come to faith. You just have to say, 'The weight of the evidence seems to show this is true, so even though I don't have answers to all my questions, I'm going to believe—and then hope for answers in the long run.' That's what happened with me."

"Do I have to put my mind on hold in order to believe something as unlikely as miracles?"

Bill looked me straight in the eye. "Only if you believe that God does not exist!" he stressed. "Then I would agree—miracles would be absurd. But *if* there is a Creator who designed and brought the universe into being, who sustains it moment by moment, who is responsible for the very natural laws that govern the physical world, then it's certainly rational to believe that miracles are possible."

"Let me get this straight," I prodded. "You're saying that if there is no God, then miracles don't make sense."

"Right," Bill agreed. "A miracle is something that is not produced by natural causes. If you deny the existence of supernatural causes—if you deny the existence of God—then you have to say miracles can't happen."

"Which is exactly what many people do say," I agreed. "But if there is a God," I continued slowly, still trying to make sense of this idea, "then miracles do not contradict science?"

"Exactly!" Bill beamed. "Because if God exists, then he is responsible for natural law, and he can intervene to perform miracles." (See the box "Quote to Consider: Miracles & the Laws of Nature.")

TOP FIVE REASONS TO GIVE GOD THE BENEFIT OF THE DOUBT

I understood Bill's point: that *if* God exists, then it's reasonable to believe that miracles are possible. But to many people, that's a pretty big *if.* The big question, of course, is whether it's rational to believe in the existence of God. When I asked Bill to give me some reasons for believing, he offered me five off the top of his head.

Reason #1: God Makes Sense of the Universe's Origin

Nearly every scientist agrees that the universe had a beginning. The most widely accepted explanation is the "Big Bang" theory or some variation of it. The question is: *What made the bang?*

If you hear a noise, you look for the cause of that noise, right? So think about it: If there must be a cause for a little bang, then doesn't it also make sense that there would be a cause for a big bang?

Quotes to Consider

Big Bang

Almost everyone now believes that the universe, and time itself, had a beginning at the Big Bang.

STEPHEN HAWKING, PHYSICIST

Suppose you suddenly hear a loud bang . . . and you ask me, "What made that bang?" and I reply, "Nothing, it just happened." You would not accept that.

KAI NIELSON, PHILOSOPHER

Reason #2: God Makes Sense of the Universe's Complexity

In the past 35 years, scientists have been stunned to discover that the universe is finely tuned to an incomprehensible precision to support life. (Check out the box "Random Chance?") For many scientists, this points in a very compelling way toward the existence of an Intelligent Designer. (You can read more about what scientists think about this Intelligent Designer in the chapter on Objection #3, evolution.)

Random Chance?

Here are some of the data gathered by scientists—both Christians and non-Christians—that point toward complexity and orderedness at the beginning of the universe:

- Stephen Hawking has calculated that if the rate of the universe's expansion one second after the Big Bang had been smaller by even one part in a hundred thousand million million, the universe would have collapsed into a fireball.

- British physicist P. C. W. Davies has concluded that the odds against the initial conditions being suitable for the formation of stars—which are necessary for planets and thus life—is a one followed by at least a thousand billion billion zeroes.

- Davies also estimated that if the strength of gravity were changed by only one part in 10^{100}, life could never have developed. (For comparison, there are only 10^{80} atoms in the entire known universe.)

- There are about 50 constants and quantities—for example, the amount of usable energy in the universe, the difference in mass between protons and neutrons, the proportion of matter to antimatter—that must be balanced to a mathematically infinitesimal degree for any life to be possible.

Reason #3: God Makes Sense of Moral Values

A third piece of evidence pointing toward God is the existence of "objective moral values." By that, philosophers mean that certain things are right—or wrong—whether or not everyone believes them to be right or wrong.

For example, to say the Holocaust was "objectively wrong" is to say it was wrong even though the Nazis thought it was right. And it would still be wrong even if the Nazis had won WWII and succeeded in brainwashing or exterminating everyone who disagreed with them.

So what does this have to do with the existence of God? I would never agree, for instance, that an atheist can't have moral values or live a basically ethical life. I have friends who don't believe in God and who are as kind and caring as some of the Christians I know.

The question is not, Can atheists have moral values? The question is, Where do objective moral values come from?

If there is no God, Bill Craig explained, then morality is just a matter of personal taste—something like saying, "Broccoli tastes good." Well, it tastes good to some people but bad to others. There isn't any objective truth to that; it's a subjective opinion. And to say that killing innocent children is wrong would be just an expression of taste, saying, "I don't like the killing of innocent children—I find it unpleasant."

Quote to Consider

I think you share my profound belief that there are indeed some moral absolutes. When it comes to torture, to government-sanctioned murder, to "disappearances" . . . these are outrages against all of us.

JOHN HEALEY, EXECUTIVE DIRECTOR OF AMNESTY INTERNATIONAL

Would it be possible for objective moral values to exist *apart* from the existence of God? In other words, could there be objective moral values even if God does not exist? You could argue, for instance, that objective moral values are merely the products of evolution—that a moral atrocity such as rape became an atrocity because it does not help the human species and therefore came to be viewed as wrong. Most people would, I think, be uncomfortable with the implications of that argument—what would happen if, for some reason, rape became advantageous for the survival of the species? Would it then become morally right? Our very discomfort with such a thought is in itself an argument for some far deeper, more absolute source of objective morality.

The question is, Do objective moral values really exist? Ask yourself: "Is torturing a child for fun *ever* morally justifiable?" If you say no, then deep down you hold some objective moral values. You may have your own ideas about why this is so, but one theory that makes sense of the existence of moral values is that they come from God.

Reason #4: God Makes Sense of the Resurrection

At about this point in Bill's top-five list, I started to feel like we'd gotten away from the subject of miracles.

"True," he admitted. "But my argument is that if we have good reasons to believe in God, then we *can* believe in miracles. That's why I've been giving reasons that point toward God's existence."

I nodded, but I still wanted to get back to miracles themselves.

"Well," Bill continued, "miracles themselves can be part of the case for God's existence. Consider the Resurrection, for instance. If Jesus of Nazareth really did come back from the dead, then we have a divine miracle on our hands—and pretty powerful evidence for the existence of God."

I asked Bill to recap what he considers the strongest historical evidence for Christ's resurrection—"But," I stressed, "don't assume that the New Testament is the inspired word of God."

For the purposes of his answer, he agreed to consider the New Testament to be simply a collection of first-century documents that can be subjected to analysis like any other ancient records. And he gave me four facts that are accepted by historians from a broad spectrum. (See the box "Four Facts.")

"Okay, then," I asked Bill. "What do you think is the best explanation for these four facts?"

"Personally," he answered, "I think the very best explanation is the same one provided by eyewitnesses: That God raised Jesus from the dead."

Four Facts

1. The location of Jesus' burial was widely known and agreed on. No competing stories contradict what the Bible says about this, and it's reported in very early information that came too soon for it to be based on legend.
2. The Sunday after the crucifixion, Jesus' tomb was found empty. Both Jesus' followers and those who denied that Jesus could be raised (like the Jewish leaders and the Roman soldiers guarding the tomb) agree on the fact that the tomb was empty.
3. On multiple occasions and under various circumstances, different individuals and groups of people experienced appearances of Jesus alive again—after the tomb was found empty.
4. The original disciples suddenly and sincerely came to believe that Jesus was risen from the dead—sincerely enough to be willing to die for that belief.

(If you're interested in a more detailed exploration of whether or not Jesus rose from the dead, you can find it in *The Case for Christ* and *The Case for Christ—Student Edition.*)

Reason #5: God Can Be Immediately Experienced

"Lee," Bill said, "can you prove that the external world exists?"

The question caught me off guard. I thought about it for a moment, but for every proof I could think of, I could think of an argument Bill might throw back at me. "I know it exists, but I'm not sure how I would prove it," I finally conceded.

"Right," Bill said with approval. "After all, you could be a brain in a vat being stimulated with electrodes by a mad scientist so that you just think you're seeing an external world." When he saw the look I gave him, he added, "But you'd have to be crazy to think that. So you're right to believe that the world exists, even if you can't prove it. It's still a rational belief because it's based on your experience."

"Okay," I said, wondering what all this had to do with God and miracles.

"In the same way, it's rational to believe in God if you've had an experience with God," Bill explained. "And I've had such an experience. God invaded my life when I was 16 years old, and for more than 30 years I've walked with him day by day, year by year, as a living reality in my experience. In the absence of overwhelming arguments for atheism—and in light of the powerful case for God and Christianity—it's perfectly rational to go on believing in the reality of that experience."

A KNOCK ON THE DOOR

I wanted to get to the heart of the confidence Bill had in what he was saying.

"As you sit here right now, deep in your soul, do you know for a fact that Christianity is true?" I asked.

Without hesitating, he replied, "Yes, I do."

"How do you know for sure?"

"Ultimately, the way a Christian really knows that Christianity is true is through God's Spirit," he said. "The Holy Spirit whispers to our spirit that we belong to God." Bill thought for a moment, then said, "Let's say you're going to school to see if the dean is in. You see his car in the parking lot. You ask the secretary if he's in, and she says, 'Yes, I just spoke with him.' You see light from under his office door. You listen and hear his voice on the telephone. On the basis of all this evidence, you have good reasons to conclude that the dean is in his office.

"But you could do something quite different. You could go to the door and knock on it and meet the dean face-to-face. At that point, the evidence of the car in the parking lot, the secretary's statement, the light under the door, the voice on the telephone—all of that would still be valid, but it wouldn't be the main evidence, because now you've met the dean face-to-face.

"And in the same way, when we've met God, so to speak, face-to-face, all of the arguments and evidence for his existence—though they're still perfectly valid—take second place. They now become confirmatory of what God himself has shown us through the witness of the Holy Spirit in our hearts."

I thought for a moment, then asked, "And this immediate experience of God is available to anyone who looks for it?"

"Absolutely. The Bible says God is knocking on the door of our life, and if we open it we will encounter him and experience him personally. We've been talking a lot about miracles today," Bill said. "It's no exaggeration to say that knowing God personally and seeing him change lives are the greatest miracles of all."

Because of my own experience with God after years of living as an atheist, I know he was right.

Based on how God has transformed my life, my attitudes, my relationships, my motivations, my marriage, and my priorities through his very real presence in my life, I have to say that miracles like manna from heaven, the virgin birth, and the Resurrection—well, they're child's play for a God like that.

OBJECTION #3:

Evolution Explains Life, So God Isn't Needed

Charles Darwin didn't want to murder God, as he once put it. But he did.

Time magazine

f you'd asked me about Darwin when I was 14 years old, I would have agreed with *Time* magazine—God was dead, and Darwin's theory of evolution had killed him—at least for me.

I was sitting in biology class at Prospect High School in Mount Prospect, Illinois, when I first learned about evolution. My teacher explained that life originated millions of years ago when chemicals randomly reacted with each other in a warm ocean on the primordial earth. Then, through a process of survival of the fittest and natural selection, life forms gained in complexity. Eventually, human beings emerged from the same family tree as apes.

Although the teacher didn't address this aspect of evolution, its biggest implication was obvious to me: If evolution explains the origin and development of life, then God was out of a job! What did we need God for? Life was just the natural result of the random interaction of chemicals.

SCIENCE VS. RELIGION?

But is Darwinism true? I walked away from my formal education convinced it was. As my spiritual journey began taking me deeper into science, though, I started to have an increasingly uneasy feeling. The more I investigated the issue, the more I saw that I might have overlooked some important information. I began to question whether the conclusions of Darwinism are really justified by the hard scientific facts.

This is not, I soon discovered, a case of religion vs. science. Instead, this is an issue of science vs. science. More and more biologists, biochemists, and other researchers—not just Christians—have raised serious objections to the theory of evolution in recent years. They claim that its assumptions are sometimes based on flimsy, incomplete, or flawed data.

I had been more than happy, as a teenager, to latch on to Darwinism as an excuse to abandon the idea of God. But someone who knows me well once described me as being "a sucker for truth." My training in journalism and law compels me to dig beneath opinion and theories, all the way down until I hit the bedrock of solid facts.

In this chapter, you'll find some of the information I uncovered in my investigation. I'm not going to try to make up your mind for you. I went that route in biology class years ago, and I'm not going to blindly accept anyone else's conclusions again—or force my own conclusions on anyone either. But at the end of this chapter I'll tell you what I think as a result of my exploration of these issues; by then you may have come to some conclusions of your own.

MICRO- VS. MACRO-EVOLUTION

Everyone agrees that evolution is true to some extent. Undeniably, there are variations *within* species of animals and plants, which explains why there are more than 200 different varieties of dogs, why cows can be bred for improved milk production, and why bacteria can adapt and develop immunity to antibiotics. This is called "micro-evolution."

But Darwin's theory goes much further than that, claiming that life began with simple, single-cell creatures and then developed through mutation (accidental changes) and natural selection (changes that helped the species survive) into the huge variety of plant and animal life now in existence. Human beings came on the scene from the same common ancestor as the ape. Scientists call this more controversial theory "macro-evolution."

For Quick Reference

micro-evolution = gradual changes *within* a species (for example, over several generations of dogs)

macro-evolution = gradual change from one species to another (for example, from fish to amphibian to reptile)

Based on observations of changes *within* species (for example, the fact that bacteria can develop into drug-resistant forms), Darwin theorized that evolution occurred *across* species (in other words, that over time an amoeba would evolve into a complex sea creature into a land creature, and so on). Darwin himself said that the lack of fossil evidence showing animals evolving from one species into another "is perhaps the most obvious and serious objection" to his theory, but he confidently predicted that such fossil evidence would be discovered in the future.

Fast-forward to 1979. David M. Raup, curator of the Field Museum of Natural History in Chicago, said, "We are now about one hundred and twenty years after Darwin and the knowledge of the fossil record has been greatly expanded. We now have a quarter of a million fossil species, but the situation hasn't changed much. . . . We have even fewer examples of evolutionary transition than we had in Darwin's time."

What the fossil evidence *does* show is that in rocks dated back some 575 million years, there is a sudden appearance of nearly all the animal phyla currently known, and they appear fully formed, not in various evolutionary stages.

ORIGIN OF LIFE

A bigger question than how different species developed is how life itself began. Macro-evolution theorizes that single-cell organisms developed into all the life forms that we now know. But where did those single-cell organisms come from? How did life begin in the first place?

Darwin speculated that nonliving chemicals, given the right amount of time and the right environment, could develop by themselves into living matter. In Darwin's day, scientific observation was less precise than it is now, and the idea of life developing on its own seemed natural enough. People once thought that maggots developed spontaneously from rotting meat, and that view of how life developed fit with Darwin's speculation.

When Francesco Redi showed that meat developed maggots only when it was exposed to flies who could lay the eggs from which maggots hatch, the idea of life developing on its own seemed less likely. But in the 1920s the idea became popular again. And in 1953 two scientists, Stanley Miller and Harold Urey, conducted an experiment at the University of Chicago that seemed to confirm the theory of life developing from nonliving chemicals.

Miller-Urey Experiment

Miller and Urey re-created what they considered to be the atmosphere of the primitive earth (methane, ammonia, hydrogen, and water) in a laboratory and shot electricity through it to simulate the effects of lightning.

Before long, they found that some amino acids—the building blocks of life—had been created.

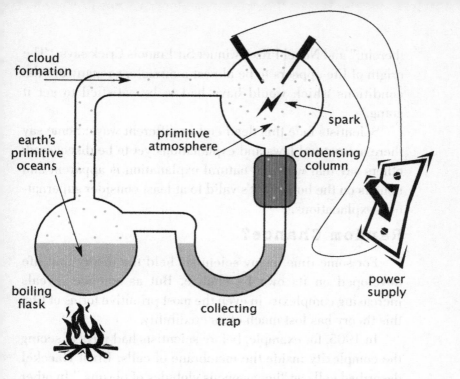

This experiment created a stir within the science community. Scientists became optimistic that the questions about the origin of life would be solved within a few decades. But this has not been the case.

More Recent Theories

More recent scientific thought suggests that natural theories of life arising on its own no longer appear valid. For instance, since 1980, NASA scientists have shown that primitive earth did not have methane, ammonia, or hydrogen (the components of the Miller-Urey experiment) in any significant amounts. Without those gases, the experiment does not work.

In fact, British astrophysicist Fred Hoyle compares the likelihood of life appearing on Earth by chemical reactions as "equivalent to the possibility that a tornado sweeping through a junkyard might assemble a Boeing 747 from the materials therein," and Nobel Prize—winner Sir Francis Crick says, "The origin of life appears to be almost a miracle, so many are the conditions which would have had to be satisfied to get it going."

Scientists face this dead end in different ways: Some say there are natural laws and explanations yet to be discovered; others say that when no natural explanation is apparent and none is on the horizon, it's valid to at least consider supernatural explanations.

Random Chance?

For some time, many scientists held the theory that life developed on its own by chance. But as science reveals increasing complexity in even the most primitive forms of life, this theory has lost much of its credibility.

In 1905, for example, before scientists had ways of seeing the complexity inside the membrane of cells, Ernst Haeckel described cells as "homogenous globules of plasma." In other words, blobs that are the same all the way through.

Recently one scientist very creatively—but quite accurately—described a single-cell organism as a high-tech factory, complete with artificial languages and decoding systems; central memory banks that store and retrieve impressive amounts of information; precision control systems that regulate the automatic assembly of components; proofreading and quality control mechanisms that safeguard against errors; assembly systems that use principles of refabrication and modular construction; and a complete replication system that allows the organism to duplicate itself at bewildering speeds.

The statistical odds of developing even the most basic living cell by chance are astronomical. I talked about this with origin-of-life scientist Walter Bradley, who pointed out that it takes about 100 of the right amino acids lined up in the right manner to make one protein molecule. And that's just the first step. Creating one protein molecule doesn't mean you've created life. Now you have to bring together a collection of protein molecules—maybe 200 of them—with just the right functions to get one typical living cell.

"The mathematical odds of assembling a living organism are so astronomical that nobody still believes that random chance accounts for the origin of life," Dr. Bradley told me. "Even if you optimized the conditions, it wouldn't work. If you took all the carbon in the universe and put it on the face of the earth, allowed it to chemically react at the most rapid rate possible, and left it for a billion years, the odds of creating just one functional protein molecule would be one chance in a 10 with 60 zeroes after it."

Even if amino acids could have been naturally produced, as the Miller-Urey experiment claimed, there's no explanation for how they could have become assembled into a living cell by themselves. *That's* the real challenge—and one that scientists have been unable to explain. No hypothesis, such as there must be some kind of natural attraction between amino acids, has stood up to scrutiny.

That's why some scientists—both Christian and non-Christian—are concluding that the orderliness and complexity of life points not to random chance but to an intelligent design in both the origin and development of life.

AN INTELLIGENT DESIGNER?

The obvious question—for me at least—is, Where does this intelligent design come from? Does the evidence for an intelligent design imply that there is an Intelligent Designer?

I think of it this way. Every time I've come across written communication—whether it's a painting on a cave wall or a novel from Amazon.com or the words "I love you" inscribed in the sand on the beach—there has always been someone who did the writing. Even if I can't see the couple who wrote

"I love you," I don't assume that the words randomly appeared by chance or the movement of the waves. Someone of intelligence made that written communication.

And what is encoded on the DNA inside every cell of every living creature is purely and simply written information. (I'm not saying this because I'm a writer; scientists will tell you this.) We use a 26-letter alphabet in English; in DNA, there is a four-letter chemical alphabet, whose letters combine in various sequences to form all the instructions needed to guide the functioning of the cell.

Each cell in the human body contains more information than in all 30 volumes of the *Encyclopaedia Britannica*. For me, that's reason enough to believe this isn't the random product of unguided nature, but it's the unmistakable sign of an Intelligent Designer.

SCIENTIFICALLY INFORMED FAITH

Do you have to give up science to believe in God? Here's what James Tour, a nanoscientist on the cutting edge of molecular theory, says about that: "I stand in awe of God because of what he has done through his creation. Only a rookie who knows nothing about science would say science takes away from faith. If you really study science, it will bring you closer to God."

How ironic, I thought. Once, a limited understanding of evolutionary science had pushed me toward atheism. Now, an increasing grasp of molecular science was cementing my confidence in God.

Time magazine was wrong: Darwin didn't murder God. He just couldn't read God's writing.

Other Resources on This Topic:

If you're interested in a more detailed discussion of this topic, you'll find an extended interview with Dr. Bradley in the longer edition of *The Case for Faith.* You may also find these books interesting:

- Charles B. Thaxton, Walter L. Bradley, and Roger L. Olsen. *The Mystery of Life's Origin.* Dallas: Lewis and Stanley, 1984.
- Phillip E. Johnson. *Darwin on Trial,* 2d ed. Downers Grove, Ill.: InterVarsity Press, 1993.
- William A. Dembski, ed. *Mere Creation.* Downers Grove, Ill.: InterVarsity Press, 1998.
- J. P. Moreland, ed. *The Creation Hypothesis.* Downers Grove, Ill.: InterVarsity Press, 1994.
- Michael J. Behe. *Darwin's Black Box.* New York: Free Press, 1996.
- Michael Denton. *Evolution: A Theory in Crisis.* Chevy Chase, Md.: Adler & Adler, 1986.
- Hank Hanegraaf. *The Face That Demonstrates the Farce of Evolution.* Nashville: Word, 1998.

It's Intolerant to Claim Jesus Is the Only Way to God

A reporter for one of the network news programs called to ask me about the growing interest in spirituality around the country. We had a pleasant conversation for a while—until I said it was my hope that everyone experimenting with various beliefs would eventually meet Jesus.

Instantly the conversation turned cold. "Are you telling me that two-thirds of the world is going to hell because they don't believe in Jesus?" he angrily demanded. His tone of voice made it clear that he thought I was narrow-minded and intolerant.

Ultimately, though, his problem isn't with me. It's with Jesus. Because one of Jesus' most outrageous claims is this: "I am the way and the truth and the life. No one comes to the Father except through me" (John 14:6).

As I explored Christianity, this was the statement I found most offensive. It's one thing to claim to be *a* way to God—but *the* way? That sounds pretty intolerant!

ALONE IN INTOLERANCE?

Other religions—many of them, anyway—seem at first glance to be much more tolerant. When I was in India, I told some Hindus that Jesus is the Son of God, and they replied, "No problem!"

I was surprised. "You're saying that you accept the fact that Jesus Christ is the Son of God?" I asked.

"Sure," they said. "We have millions of gods. There's no problem adding Jesus."

But when I said, "No, you don't understand—Jesus said he's the *only* Son of God, and the *only* path that leads to eternal life," that's when they got mad. That was a statement they couldn't tolerate.

I asked Ravi Zacharias, who grew up in India with Hindu, Muslim, Buddhist, and Sikh friends, how he felt about the intolerance of Christianity's claims.

"If Christianity is intolerant," he said, "then so are other religions. All religions find things they can't accept in other religions." He ran down a list of examples:

- Muslims cannot tolerate disagreement with the Koran.
- Buddhism does not accept the Hindu scriptures and the Hindu caste system.
- Hinduism does not accept views of life that do not include karma and reincarnation.
- Atheists cannot accept any belief in God.

REMEMBER THE ELEPHANT?

But even if other religions aren't necessarily any more tolerant than Christianity, who's to say one of them might not be valid? Or maybe all of them, in some way?

Some people say that when you strip away all the nonessentials, all the world religions are essentially the same. That would mean that all the world's faith systems are equally valid. But Ravi's quick summary of different beliefs in the list above suggests that religions *aren't* all the same. Some of the world's religions teach quite different things about the existence of God himself. (See the chart "God or No God?")

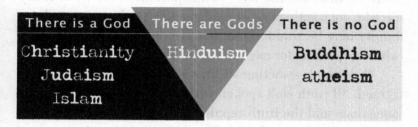

God or No God?

There is a God	There are Gods	There is no God
Christianity	Hinduism	Buddhism
Judaism		atheism
Islam		

Still, even if the different religions don't teach the same thing, a popular thought today is that each religion has a slice of the truth. For a Buddhist, Buddhism is truth as he or she perceives it. Hinduism is true for a Hindu.

Maybe you know the old story of the three blind men feeling the elephant. One man feels the elephant's leg and says, "Aha! This is a tree." But the second guy gets hold of the elephant's ear and says, "No way! It's a big fan." The third man, holding the elephant's tail, says, "You're both wrong! This is clearly a rope."

I asked Ravi, "Isn't it possible that the world's religions are like the blind men and the elephant? That each one has a different but valid response to who God is?"

Ravi shook his head. "The blind man may tell you it's a tree, but he's wrong. It is not a tree or a rope or a fan. The seeing man knows this is an elephant," he said. "He knows the truth; his sight has revealed it to him."

MANY TRUTHS?

Would it be intolerant to tell the blind men that they were mistaken? What if they said, "It may be true for you that this is an elephant, but for me it's true that it's a rope"?

Claiming exclusive insight on truth is pretty offensive these days. But logically it makes sense that if atheism or Buddhism—which say there is no God—are true, then Christianity or Islam—which say there *is* a God—*cannot* be true. (For more on this, see the box "Schizophrenic God.") But many people, not wanting to seem judgmental, prefer to say, "Christianity may be true for you, but Hinduism [or Buddhism or whatever] is true for me."

"I do think sometimes Christians are judgmental," Ravi agreed. "If truth isn't spoken with love, it makes the speaker obnoxious and the truth repulsive. Mahatma Gandhi said, 'I like their Christ, but I don't like their Christians.' Christianity's history has some explaining to do." (See the timeline, "When Religion Turns Ugly," on pp. 56–57.)

"On the other hand," Ravi continued, "it is possible to lovingly claim that something is the only truth, just as a scientist can very gently say, 'This is the second law of thermodynamics,' without adding, 'Now, can we vote on how many of us can cooperate with it?'

"Jesus Christ has made it clear that the eternal truths of God may be known. He established through his resurrection that he is the Son of God. He is the centerpiece of the gospel—in him, all of truth comes together. So while there may be aspects of truth elsewhere, the sum total of truth is in Christ."

WHY NOT JESUS?

"If Jesus is the truth, why do so many people reject him?" I asked Ravi. "If Christianity is true, you would think that people would recognize it. But statistics show that Christianity

Schizophrenic God

This question of how I could deny the validity of other religions really bothered me—until someone explained it to me this way:

"Most of the world's major religions are based on some kind of holy writings that claim to be God's revelation of himself to man. But think about it: First, God would have to go to one part of the world and tell people, 'Okay, here's who I am: I'm the Trinity—Father, Son, and Holy Spirit—and Jesus died for the sins of humankind so that people can be reconciled with me and spend eternity in heaven. Forgiveness is a free gift that cannot be earned.'

"Then God would go to another part of the world and whisper to people: 'You know that Trinity stuff? Forget it! I'm really Allah, and Muhammad is my final prophet, and forgiveness is not a free gift, but you must try to earn your way to heaven through giving alms to the poor and visiting Mecca, praying a certain number of times a day, and so forth.'

"Then God would go to another part of the world and say, 'Forget all that other stuff. I'm actually *millions* of gods. I'm good gods and bad gods, but we're impersonal deities who you can't really get to know. And you must go through a series of reincarnations to try to work off the bad karma in your life—not so you'll go to heaven, but so you'll just sort of be absorbed into the cosmos in the end.'

"And then God would go somewhere else and tell them something else about himself that's completely different. *If God were to do all of this, he'd be schizophrenic!* Then we'd *really* be in trouble!"

Somehow this explanation really clicked with me. It wouldn't make sense, if there were a God, for all those contradictory views about him to be true at the same time. One could be wholly true. Or they could all be false. But they can't all be wholly true.

isn't winning huge numbers of converts from other major world religions."

"That's a troubling question," Ravi agreed. "To look at it from another perspective, why is Buddhism so popular in America today?" he asked. "My answer is simple: because in Buddhism you can be good without having God.

"Why is Islam attractive to some? The answer to that relates to the politics of the places where Islam prospers. What about the Hindu faith? Its teachings about treating the earth with reverence are appealing today."

"Why not Christ?" I asked.

"Because he calls you to die to yourself," he replied. "Whenever truth involves a total commitment, people resist. Christ demands more than most people are willing to give."

Given the level of commitment that Christianity requires, I was curious about what prompted Ravi to respond to the message of Jesus. "Tell me a bit of your story," I said.

Timeline: When Religion Turns Ugly

1095–1291
The Crusades
The Pope sends Crusaders to reclaim the Holy Land from Muslims. Over the next two centuries, Crusaders slaughter not only Muslims but also Middle Eastern Christians. Some believe they are doing God's will; some are out for personal gain. Other Christians, hearing of the bloodshed, refuse to support the Crusades.

about 30 A.D.
Jesus warns that there will always be those who claim to be Christians but are not authentic Christians (Matthew 7:21–23).

1163, 1472, 1542
The Inquisition
Intended at first to protect the faith against heresy (false teaching), the Inquisition develops into a reign of political terror in which the victims were burned at the stake.

The Case for Faith

RAVI'S STORY

"In India, you are what you are born into," Ravi told me. "My father and my mother were considered Christians, even though they didn't really believe or practice Christianity. The reason they were Christians was simply because they were not Buddhists, Muslims, or Hindus. I don't remember ever hearing about Jesus at my church, which was very liberal-minded.

"Just before I came to Christ, my sisters heard the gospel and made their commitment. I came to believe in Jesus in two stages. The first stage was when I heard about Jesus in an auditorium when I was 17. I said to myself, 'Something about this is true and I want it.' I went forward and was counseled about becoming a Christian, but I didn't really understand."

Life with No Meaning

"At the time, I was under a lot of pressure in a culture where academic performance was extremely important. If you

---

1692
Salem Witch Trials
Nineteen accused witches are hanged; one is pressed to death; 17 more accused witches die in prison. Ultimately, it was a Christian named Increase Mather who spoke out and helped bring the trials to an end.

2000—
Confession
Pope John Paul II publicly confesses and asks God's forgiveness for the sins committed or condoned by the Roman Catholic Church over the last two millennia.

1940s
Holocaust
Against all biblical teaching, Hitler claims to be acting on behalf of the Christian faith in exterminating Jews. Much of the church fails to resist, but some Christian leaders speak out against Hitler; some (like Dietrich Bonhoeffer) are put to death.

Today
Questioners ask whether abuses in church history are valid reasons to reject Jesus Christ, or whether it's fair to blame Christianity for the actions of those who claim to follow Jesus but whose hurtful behavior violates all that Jesus taught.

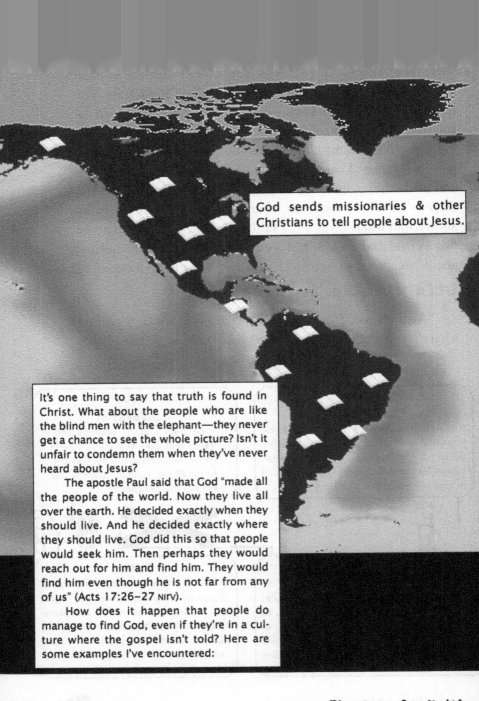

God sends missionaries & other Christians to tell people about Jesus.

It's one thing to say that truth is found in Christ. What about the people who are like the blind men with the elephant—they never get a chance to see the whole picture? Isn't it unfair to condemn them when they've never heard about Jesus?

The apostle Paul said that God "made all the people of the world. Now they live all over the earth. He decided exactly when they should live. And he decided exactly where they should live. God did this so that people would seek him. Then perhaps they would reach out for him and find him. They would find him even though he is not far from any of us" (Acts 17:26–27 NIrV).

How does it happen that people do manage to find God, even if they're in a culture where the gospel isn't told? Here are some examples I've encountered:

The Case for Faith

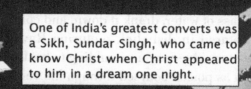

One of India's greatest converts was a Sikh, Sundar Singh, who came to know Christ when Christ appeared to him in a dream one night.

A Muslim woman in a Muslim country felt lost and empty. One day, out of the blue, she said, "Jesus, can you help me?" She stopped in her tracks and asked herself, "Why did I name *him?*" That woman ended up becoming a Christian. God saw a heart that hungered for him and broke past the barriers of her environment.

Virtually every Muslim who has come to follow Christ has done so either because of the love of Christ expressed through a Christian or because of a vision, dream, or some other supernatural intervention. No religion has a more intricate doctrine of visions than Islam, and it's amazing that God uses that sensitivity to the supernatural world to reveal himself.

weren't at the top of the class, then you weren't going to succeed. I couldn't cope with it. I also had a very strict father, and I struggled with that. I received a lot of physical punishment.

"A few months later, I decided to end my own life. I was not depressed; my friends would have been shocked to hear that I was planning to commit suicide. But for me, life had no meaning or purpose. I went to school one day and used the keys to the science lab to check out some poisons. I put them in a glass of water, drank it down, and collapsed to my knees."

I stared in disbelief, picturing Ravi as a confused and hope-starved teenager crumbling to his knees and gasping for breath as poison coursed through his veins.

"I was rushed to the hospital," Ravi continued, "where they emptied all the poisons out of me. If no one had found me, I would be dead. As I lay in bed, a friend walked in with a New Testament and showed me John 14. I couldn't hold the book; I was too dehydrated. My mother had to read it to me."

A Second Chance at Life

"There she was, reading where Jesus was talking to Thomas and saying, 'I am the way, the truth, and the life. No one comes to the Father except through me.' Then she came to verse 19, where Jesus tells his disciples, 'Because I live, you also will live.'

"That verse touched my soul. I said in a prayer, 'Jesus, I don't know much about you, but you are telling me you're the source of true life.' I didn't understand the concept of sin. In that culture, I couldn't have. But what I did understand was that he was offering himself to me to give me life.

"So I said, 'If you take me out of this hospital room, I will leave no stone unturned in my search for truth.' And I walked out of that room five days later an absolutely brand-new man. I began to study the Bible, and it dramatically changed my life. My brothers and sisters also came to follow Jesus, and so did my parents before they died.

The Case for Faith

"But it was in that hospital room that Christ told me—simply through the words of Scripture, with no explanation provided by anyone—that he could give me what life was really meant to be. Years of study have only confirmed my decision to follow him. I took some philosophy courses at Cambridge under a famous atheist, and I remember thinking in astonishment, 'These are the best arguments atheists have?' It merely confirmed the truth of Scripture."

LOOK FOR YOURSELF

"What would you tell someone wondering about Jesus now?" I asked.

"The Bible says, 'When you look for me with all your heart, you will find me' (Jeremiah 29:13 NIrV). Think about that—that's an amazing promise! For any genuine person who brings an unprejudiced view, I don't see how he or she can come away from an examination of the claims for Christ without saying that there is nothing like this on the face of the earth.

"I've traveled the world. I've searched high and low. I've found nothing that satisfies my mind, my heart, and the deepest longing of my soul like Jesus does. He is not only the way, the truth, and the life; he is personal to me. He is *my* way, and *my* truth, and *my* life—just as he can be for anyone who reaches out to him."

A Loving God Would Never Send People to Hell

hen I have tough questions about God, often I seek out my friend J. P. Moreland. He's trained in philosophy and science, but he's also one of those rare people who can explain difficult things in everyday language. Since the concept of hell is so troubling, I went to him for a long conversation that I'll distill into some Q and A's.

Q: How could a loving God torture people forever?

A: For one thing, hell isn't a torture chamber. Hell is, first of all, about relationships—broken relationships. The Christian faith says that people matter intensely to God. If people matter, then so do relationships.

In the Bible, hell is separation or banishment from the most beautiful being in the world—God himself. It's exclusion not only from God but also from those who have come to know and love him.

Q: Is hell a punishment for having broken God's standards, or is it a natural consequence of choosing to be separate from God?

A: It's both. Make no mistake: hell *is* punishment—but it's not a punish*ing*. It's not torture. The punishment of hell is separation from God and the shame, anguish, and regret that go along with it. The pain may be both mental and physical, but it will be the pain and sorrow of final, unending banishment from God and the good life for which we were created. Hell is the final sentence that says you refused regularly to live in relationship with God, and the inevitable result of that choice is to be sent away from God for all eternity. So it *is* punishment. But it's also the natural consequence of a life that has been lived in a certain direction.

Q: Is hell a physical place?

A: Yes. The Bible says that our bodies will be raised and our souls rejoined with them at the final judgment. Hell will need to be a physical place to house those physical bodies.

Q: Will people burn in flames in hell?

A: I believe that the imagery of flames the Bible uses to describe hell is a figure of speech. Trying to take the flames of hell literally results in nonsense. For example, hell is described as a place of utter darkness. How can that be? Flames would light things up.

Here's a similar example: The Bible says that, at his return, Christ will come surrounded by flames and with a big sword coming out of his mouth. Will he be unable to speak because he's choking on a sword? Few people consider that to be a literal sword. Instead, the sword in that passage of Scripture is an image that stands for the word of God. The flames stand for Christ coming in judgment.

Another example: In Hebrews 12:29, God is called a consuming fire. Yet nobody thinks God is a cosmic Bunsen burner. Using the flame imagery is a way of saying he's a God of judgment.

Q: What about hell being a place where worms constantly eat people's flesh?

The Case for Faith

A: In Jesus' day, thousands of animals were sacrificed every week in the Temple, and there was a sewage system for the blood and fat to flow outside, where it gathered in a pool. There would have been worms and maggots constantly feeding on that waste. It must have been a very ugly—and smelly—place. When Jesus was teaching, he used this metaphor as a way of saying hell is worse than that disgusting place outside the city, a place all of his listeners would have known about.

Q: Doesn't the phrase "gnashing of teeth" used to describe hell mean that people are in pain and torture?

A: "Gnashing of teeth" is an expression of rage at realizing you've just made a huge mistake. When you hear about people grinding their teeth or gritting their teeth today, it means they're angry or frustrated, not that they are being tortured. If you've ever been around people who are really self-centered, you know they get angry when they don't get their way. I believe the gnashing of teeth mentioned in Scripture is an expression of the personality of the type of people who will end up in hell.

Q: If hell isn't literally a fiery place with flesh-eating worms, what's so bad about being there?

A: Any figure of speech has a literal point. What is figurative is the burning flame. What is literal is that this is a place of utter heartbreak. It's a loss of everything. The Bible is trying to communicate that hell is the worst possible situation a person could ever find himself in.

Q: If the people in hell are self-absorbed and self-centered, is it possible that for them, heaven would be hell?

A: Let me put it this way: Have you ever been around somebody who was unbelievably good-looking, extremely attractive, and a lot smarter than you? When the two of you are in a group of people, the others will want to listen to him, not you. Suppose you don't care for that person, but you're kept in a room with him 24 hours a day for 30 years. That would be unbelievably difficult, even maddening.

Now, multiply those qualities 10,000 times, and you'll get just a hint of what God is like. He knows everything. He's very attractive. He's morally pure. And if people do not fall passionately in love with him, then to force them to have to be around him forever—doing the kinds of things that people who love him would want to do—would make them miserable.

Experience tells me that a person's character is not formed all at once. It's formed by thousands of little choices we each make every day. Each day we're preparing ourselves either for being with God and his people and valuing the things he values, or choosing not to engage with those things. So, yes, hell is primarily a place for people who would not want to go to heaven.

Q: If hell is for people who would not want to go to heaven, do people consciously choose hell?

A: I don't believe that they consciously reject heaven and choose to go to hell instead. But they do choose not to care about the values God encourages us to live by here on earth, and that will also be in effect in heaven.

Q: How can God send children to hell?

A: It's hard to know exactly how to think about people's ages in eternity. Will people be the age they were when they died? When they were at their physical and mental peak? Or is age irrelevant after death? Some people think that everyone will be the equivalent of an adult, so there won't be any children in either heaven or hell.

Even if you're not sure how the whole child/adult thing works out after death, one thing that's certain is this: There will be *no one* in hell who, if they had a chance to grow up to be adults, would have ended up going to heaven. *No one* will go to hell simply because all they needed was a little more time to turn toward God.

Q: Why does everyone suffer the same in hell? That doesn't seem fair. Shouldn't people like Hitler suffer more?

A: The Bible teaches that there are different degrees of suffering in hell. One passage you can read about that is Matthew 11:20–24. Jesus says people will be sentenced according to how they lived. There will be degrees of separation, isolation, and emptiness in hell. God's justice is proportional. There is not exactly the same experience for everyone.

God—a Baby Killer?

If the question of children going to **hell disturbs** you, then you may have problems with some of the accounts in the Old Testament, where God tells his people, the Israelites, to wipe out their enemies—presumably including women and children.

I sure did. Until I realized one important thing about God: *Whoever has repented, God has been willing to save.*

Think about it: When the firstborn in Egypt died, any family that followed God's directions about marking their homes were spared. God provided a way out. When Joshua attacked the city of Jericho, Rahab and her family escaped because they wanted to join the people of God. Hundreds of years before Joshua's time, God told Abraham that he'd have to wait for his claim on the land of Canaan, because God was unwilling to destroy the people living there at that time. He gave them centuries to change their violent and depraved lifestyle. The corrupt city of Nineveh repented and God saved the whole bunch.

Other details about warfare in those days help me understand God's mercy a little better. For instance, most of the time, women and children had fled before the actual fighting began. Whenever the Israelites went into an enemy city, they were first to make an offer of peace. If the people accepted it, they wouldn't be killed. The pattern is consistent: Whoever has wanted to be saved, God has saved.

Q: Why are people punished forever? Wouldn't a loving God make the punishment fit the crime by not making hell last forever?

A: This is a hard question to answer. When we think about the worst thing a person can do, usually we'll say it's harming animals or destroying the environment or hurting another person. And, no question, all of those are horrible. But I believe that truly the worst thing a person can do is to mock and dishonor and refuse to love the person that we owe absolutely everything to: God our Creator.

You see, I know from experience that God is infinitely greater in his goodness, holiness, kindness, and justice than anyone else. To think that a person could go through their whole life constantly ignoring him, constantly mocking him by the way they choose to live, saying, "I couldn't care less about what you put me here to do. I couldn't care less about your values or your Son's death for me. I'm going to ignore all that"—*that's* the ultimate sin.

And it's the only sin, when you come down to it, that lands people in hell. There will be murderers in heaven—like the apostle Paul. There will be adulterers in heaven—like King David. And liars like Abraham and cheaters like Jacob. But what you won't find in heaven is anyone who *consistently and persistently refused to have a relationship with Jesus Christ.* That's the ultimate sin. And the consequence of that is everlasting separation from God.

Q: Why doesn't God just snuff people out instead of punishing them?

A: God created people in his own image, and for that reason, people are valuable in themselves—not just because of what they do. In fact, God values people so much that he sent his Son, Jesus Christ, to suffer and die in paying for people's sins so they can spend eternity with him.

What hell does is recognize that people have value. You see, if God simply annihilated people, what he'd be saying is, "The thing that really matters is that people no longer suffer consciously, so I'm going to snuff this person out of existence in order to achieve that end." Do you see? That's treating the person as a means to an end. But people have intrinsic value. God refuses to snuff out a creature who has been made in his own image.

(There are some theologians who claim that the Bible teaches annihilation. I don't agree with them. If you want to read more about it, you can find a discussion of that subject in the longer edition of *The Case for Faith*.)

Q: If heaven is supposed to be a place without tears, then how can there be an eternal hell at the same time? Wouldn't the people in heaven mourn for those who are suffering in hell?

A: This is a painful question for me, because I know so many people who are facing an eternity without God. One thing that helps me is something the writer C. S. Lewis said: that hell doesn't have veto power over heaven. He meant that people in heaven will not be denied the privilege of enjoying their life just because they're consciously aware of hell. If the people in heaven were miserable because of loved ones in hell, then hell would have veto power over heaven.

You see, the soul is big enough to have an unperturbed sense of joy, well-being, love, and happiness, while at the same time having a sense of grief and sadness for others. Those are not inconsistent states in a person's life, and it is a mark of a person's character and maturity that he's able to have those states at the same time.

One way I personally deal with this troubling question is to do whatever I can to help the people I care about to know and love Christ, so that they won't have to face hell.

Q: Why doesn't God give people a second chance?

A: I think he does. I personally know that God gave me lots of chances in my life to get to know and follow him. But the Bible clearly says that people die only once and then face judgment.

So why doesn't God give people a second chance *after* they die? That question assumes that God didn't do everything he should have *before* people died, and I reject that. There will not be a single person who will be able to say to God, "If you had just given me another 12 months, I know I would have made that decision."

Some people think we would be more willing to follow Christ if we first died and actually experienced judgment. But I think this would be like me holding a paddle over my daughter and saying, "You *will* say you're sorry for taking your sister's CDs without asking." Any apology would not be a real apology; it would just be avoidance.

Jesus told a story about this very question, actually, in Luke 16:19–31. He said that people already have everything they need to bring them to God in this life.

Q: Wouldn't reincarnation be better than hell?

A: Usually when people ask this question they mean one of two things. First, they might mean that they like the idea of reincarnation better. But one thing I've learned is that we don't decide what's true based on what we like or don't like. We have to consider the evidence.

The second thing people might mean by this question is, "Isn't there evidence for reincarnation?" Certainly there are people who talk about memories of prior lives. Personally, I don't believe in reincarnation for at least three reasons.

1. First, it ignores what's essential to people—what makes them who they are. For instance, if you were to say, "J. P. is in the other room, and he has lost five pounds," people might say, "Good for him." What if you said, "J. P. is in the other room and guess what? He's a grasshopper." Most people would say, "That can't be J. P., because if there's one thing I know about him, it's that he's human. He's not a grasshopper." Well, reincarnation says that I could come back as a grasshopper. But if that's true, I wouldn't *be* J. P. Moreland anymore—I would be a grasshopper. My humanness is an essential part of who I am.

2. Another reason I don't believe in reincarnation is that the evidence for it—things like memories of past lives—can be explained by other means: psychological explanations, or lucky guesses, or even demonic influence.

3. Finally, I don't believe in reincarnation because there's an expert on this question, and he's Jesus of Nazareth. He's the only person in history who died, rose from the dead, and spoke authoritatively on this question. And Jesus says reincarnation doesn't happen. He says that there's only one death and after that comes the judgment.

The Case for Faith

Q: How can you love a God who sends people to hell?

A: Even after all that I've said, the idea of hell doesn't make me happy. It helps me to know that God isn't happy about hell either. Remember, he doesn't send people there; people end up there because they've chosen to live separately from God their whole lives—and when they die, that decision is sealed for eternity. But I don't feel that I have to have all the answers about hell in order to love God. Think of it this way. When you're trying to start a friendship with someone, you don't understand everything about him, and you don't necessarily agree or feel good about every view he holds. But you have to ask, on balance, do you trust this person enough to want to begin a friendship with him?

The same is true with Jesus. Not every issue will be resolved before we enter into a relationship with him. But the question is, On balance, can you trust him?

I would encourage anyone struggling with this question to read the gospel of John first and then ask, "Can I trust Jesus?" For me, the answer is yes. And I believe that, over time, as we develop our relationship with him, we'll even come to trust him in those areas that right now we don't completely understand. As the Bible says in Genesis 18:25: "Won't the Judge of the whole earth do what is right?" Ultimately, God is fair. Nobody will be able to walk away from the judgment and say, "God wasn't fair to me."

I Still Have Doubts, So I Can't Be a Christian

> Lee, I need your help. I see so many people who have such a strong faith that I feel like I don't fit in. I would like to feel confident, I wish I didn't have doubts, but I've got more questions than answers. Now I'm beginning to doubt whether I'm a Christian at all. What should I do? Could you get back to me right away?

Can you relate to that letter? I can, even though I'm the one the letter is written to—the one who's supposed to have the answers.

The truth is, I know about doubt. For much of my life I was an atheist. When I investigated Christianity, I didn't move from unbeliever to believer in a series of easy steps. I did a lot of questioning, concluding, then doubting my conclusions, and questioning all over again.

And if you think that finally becoming a Christian meant an instant end to all my questions— think again!

What about you? Do you have to answer each and every one of your questions before you can follow

Jesus? Can a person be a Christian and still have reservations or doubts? What can people do if they *want* to believe in Christ but feel that questions and doubts about Christianity are blocking their way?

If there were a one-size-fits-all answer to the problem of doubt, we wouldn't be having this conversation. The problem would be solved. Unfortunately, there's no quick and easy answer. But that doesn't mean there's no hope. Come along with me and listen to the stories of some people who've asked these same questions about faith and doubt.

THE CHURCH KID

Lynn Anderson was the son of committed Christians who were part of a small but tight-knit church in an area with few other Christians. Although he got a sense of identity and worth from his family and church community, his doubts about Christianity started early.

"Even as a little kid, I asked a lot of questions," he began. "I was always probing one level deeper, not taking anything at face value. I've never been able to totally shake that."

I smiled. I've often been accused of asking too many questions myself. "When did you become a Christian?" I asked.

"I made a profession of faith at a summer camp when I was 11, but I felt like a hypocrite afterwards. I was supposed to have committed my life to Jesus, but I wasn't even sure there *was* a Jesus. I felt like a liar."

"Did you share your feelings with anyone?"

"I talked with a minister, but he didn't seem to understand," he said. "I just kind of swallowed it. But of course I still prayed for things. I remember praying and praying that I'd get a bike and I never got one. That made me feel like God wasn't connected to me. I thought, *Let's get real. When you pray, there's nothing up there but blue sky.*"

The Case for Faith

I asked if doubt was all he felt, or if there were times when his faith felt stronger.

"Sometimes I would really sense God's presence," he told me. "I would ride home from school in a snowstorm at twilight, singing hymns and feeling I was in God's hands. But a lot of the time, I didn't believe in him—at least, not like my church friends did."

"Were you afraid they might find out?"

"Absolutely! I was scared they'd think I was bad, or be angry with me, or think my parents were spiritual failures. I was afraid my parents would be disappointed or ashamed."

"How did you feel about God at that time?" I asked.

"I told myself, *If you don't meet God's standards, you're lost—but nobody can meet those standards, especially you.* As a result, the closer I would get to God—when I'd start believing and get serious about connecting with him—the more hopeless I felt because I couldn't meet the expectations. Then I would think, *This is sick! Why would I believe in something that's going to condemn me no matter what I do? Surely, if there's a God, he couldn't be like that.*"

"What happened as you grew older?"

"I hoped this was part of being a kid. But at college, my doubts moved from being emotional to being intellectual. I found myself questioning the validity of the Bible, and I wondered why there's so much suffering in the world."

He smiled as he recalled a story. "I remember one day a student raised some huge biblical dilemma at our Christian college. The teacher couldn't answer it. Finally, after stumbling around for a while, the teacher said, 'When all the facts are in, we'll see it underscores the credibility of the Bible.'"

Anderson let out a laugh. "I remember thinking, *Oh, no! This guy's just hoping it's true, too! If you scratch under the surface, he's as scared as I am!*"

THE SMOKE SCREEN

Once Lynn was talking with a man who said, "I'm miserable. I've got a wife and kids, and I'm making more money than I can spend with both hands, and I'm sleeping with every woman in town—and I hate myself. You've got to help me, but don't give me any of that God talk because I can't believe that stuff."

They talked for hours. Finally, Lynn said, "Maybe you think you're shooting straight with me, but I'm not sure you are. I don't think your problem is that you *can't* believe; I think it's that you *won't* believe because you're afraid to give up the things that help get you through the night."

He thought for a while and then said, "Yeah, I guess that's true. I can't imagine sleeping with just one woman. I can't imagine going with less money than I make—which I'd have to do because I lie to get it." He was finally trying to be honest.

He would argue and argue for hours about his cerebral doubts. He would convince other people that he couldn't believe because he had too many objections. But they were just a smoke screen—a fog he used to hide his real hesitations about God.

I understand what that man was going through. When I was an atheist, I was pretty motivated to find faults with Christianity myself. I knew that my heavy drinking and my immoral lifestyle would have to change if I ever became a follower of Jesus, and I didn't want to let go of that. After all, it was all I knew. Sometimes, instead of trying to find the truth, I found myself *clinging* to my doubts and objections, rather than trying to find the answers to them.

If that describes you, then maybe your doubts are not so much about whether God is real. Maybe they're more about whether following Christ is worth changing your lifestyle.

Other Doubters i Have Known

Do you recognize any of these people?

The Disappointed: God hasn't answered this person's prayer or met this person's needs, so she or he wonders, *Is God really there?*

The Wounded: Abuse or rejection or some kind of suffering makes this doubter ask, "If there's a God, why does he let this happen?"

The Rebel: Wants to rebel against his or her parents, so rebels against the God they believe in.

The Independent: Says, "I'm not going to let anybody—even God—run my life or do my thinking."

The Uncommitted: Wants to keep his or her options open, so fears making a commitment to Christ.

THE WORSHIPER WITH THE BLAHS

Most people with doubts aren't looking for excuses not to believe. Most truly *do* want a stronger faith. But sometimes they end up making comparisons with the faith of others, and that can lead to doubts.

Like the young woman who said, "I hate to go to church because I hear all these people talking about wonderful things that I'm not experiencing. I believe, I study the Bible, I pray—but I don't get the joy I hear other people talking about. I don't get my prayers answered. I don't get a great sense of peace. I don't feel like I'm in the hands of a God who's guiding me down the road and is going to take care of me."

She looked up in distress and said, "Is something wrong with me, or is something wrong with God?"

WHAT FAITH ISN'T

It's easy to mix up faith and emotion. Sometimes that can leave us feeling like this young woman, desperately longing for a spiritual high—and wondering who's at fault, us or God, if we don't feel it. (That woman might do well to spend some time reading the Psalms—see the box "Beating on God's Chest"—and then see if she could answer her own question.)

Faith ≠ Feelings

Lynn Anderson—the "church kid" who struggled with doubt—shared this about faith and feelings. "I tend to be emotionally up and down. It took me years to figure out that this doesn't mean my faith is getting weaker or stronger. That's why we have to be careful about our feelings—they can be fickle.

"A guy once told me, 'I don't love my wife anymore.' My response was, 'Go home and love her.' But he said, 'You don't understand—I have no feelings for her anymore.' I said, 'I wasn't asking how you felt. I was saying, "Go home and love her."' Then he said, 'But it would be emotionally dishonest for me to treat my wife that way when I don't feel it.'

"So I asked him, 'Does your mother love you?' That seemed to insult him. He said, 'Yeah, of course.' I said, 'About three weeks after she brought you home from the hospital and you were screaming with dirty diapers and she had to wake up dog-tired and put her bare feet on the cold floor, clean up your smelly diapers, and feed you a bottle—do you think she really

---

Beating on God's Chest

When I feel as if something's missing emotionally from my faith life, I often go to the Psalms in the Old Testament of the Bible. The Psalms give quite a picture of what normal faith is like! We tend to focus on the upbeat Psalms, but did you know that 60% of them are laments, with people screaming out, "God, where are you?" Normal faith is allowed to beat on God's chest and complain. And so are you.

The Case for Faith

got a bang out of that?' He said, 'No.' I said, 'Well, then, I think your mother was being emotionally dishonest.'

"Here's the point: the measure of the mother's love wasn't that she felt good about changing the diapers, but that she was willing to do it even when she wasn't feeling particularly happy about it. And I think we need to learn that about faith. Faith is not always about having positive emotional feelings toward God or life."

Faith ≠ Lack of Doubt

Some people think that faith means a lack of doubt, but that's not true. One of my favorite Bible texts is about the man who comes to Jesus with his demon-possessed son, hoping that the boy will get healed. Jesus says all things are possible to those who believe. And the man's response is so powerful! He says, "I believe, but would you help me with my unbelief?" (You can read about it in Mark 9:14–27.)

To Think About . . .

Most people think that doubt is the opposite of faith, but it isn't. The opposite of faith is unbelief, which is a willful refusal to believe or a deliberate decision to disobey God.

I connect with that! You can have doubts even when you believe. In fact, I believe that where there are absolutely no questions, there's probably no healthy faith.

Lynn and I both get a little nervous around people with bright smiles and glassy eyes who never have a doubt in the world, who always think everything's wonderful. They don't live in the same world we do. How are they going to respond when something bad happens, challenging their rosy view of life?

How do you know your faith is strong if it has never been challenged by doubts or thoughtful questions? Doubts can help you develop a sturdier and more realistic faith.

That's what happened to me when I was a fairly new Christian and volunteered to respond to cards from church attendees who had questions. One Sunday a 12-year-old girl turned in a card that simply said she wanted to know more about Jesus.

When I called her, she asked, "Could you and your wife come have dinner with me and my dad so we could talk?"

"Of course!" I replied enthusiastically. I couldn't imagine a better way to spend an evening than telling a young person and her father about Jesus.

But when Leslie and I got to their house, I glanced at the coffee table and saw a stack of scholarly books written by critics of Christianity. It turned out that the girl's father was a scientist who had been studying critiques of the faith for a long time.

Over pizza and soft drinks, he peppered me with questions until midnight, and many of his challenges caught me completely off guard. Frankly, a few sent tremors through my faith.

I finally said, "I can't answer all your questions—but for 2,000 years people have been trying to destroy the foundations of Christianity, and I don't think that you'll be the first one to succeed. So let me do some research and get back to you."

This experience raised some doubts for me—but it also sent me into new areas of research, in which I soon found satisfying answers that boosted my confidence in Christianity. Today I'm better equipped to handle questions like those the scientist asked that night, and I'm less likely to let tough questions shake my confidence. In short, my faith is healthier for the experience.

To Think About . . .

Do you agree that a faith challenged by hard times or tough questions winds up stronger in the end?

DEALING WITH DOUBT

As for Lynn Anderson—the church kid who's struggled with doubt for as long as he can remember—doubt hasn't destroyed his faith. I asked him to share what helps him deal with doubt.

Choose to Believe

"Faith is a choice," Anderson says. "When you scratch beneath the surface, there's either a will to believe or there's a will to *not* believe. That's the core of it. And one definition of faith is that it's the will to believe. [See the box "Faith: Act of Will or Gift of God?"] It's the decision to follow the best light you have about God and not quit.

"Some people say they want to believe when they really don't. Then they make excuses for not believing. For instance, a college student told me, 'It looks to me like this whole Christian crock was invented by people who have a psychological need to believe.'

Faith: Act of Will or Gift of God?

The Bible talks about faith as a gift from God. It also talks about choosing or refusing to believe. What I learn from that is that I shouldn't get cocky and take credit for having faith, as if it's something I worked up on my own without God. (Ephesians 2:8-10 talks about this pretty plainly.) But God never withholds that gift from anyone who wants to believe, so it's not realistic to say, "I'd like to believe, but God hasn't given me faith." If you want to believe, God *will* give you faith.

"My answer was, yes, many people have a psychological need to believe—just as some people have psychological needs to *not* believe. I said to her, 'What's the reason you don't want to believe? Is it because you don't want the responsibility faith brings with it? Is it because of despair over your own faults? Or is it because you don't want to give up partying?'

"She was startled. She said, 'Who told you that? It's a little bit of all three.'

"She had reasons for not wanting to believe. Other people have different reasons. But if you're serious about dealing with doubts, you start by deciding to believe."

Go Where Faith Is

"Assuming a person wants to believe," I said, "what do you recommend as the next step?"

"I suggest they go where faith is," Lynn answered. "If you want to grow roses, you don't buy an acre at the North Pole. You go where roses grow well. If you're going to do faith, you probably don't want to join American Atheist, Inc. Get around

Other Resources on This Topic

Here are some books that might help you develop your own faith:

- Lynn Anderson. *If I Really Believe, Why Do I Have These Doubts?* Second edition. West Monroe, LA: Howard, 2000.
- Paul E. Little. *Know What You Believe.* Revised and updated. Colorado Springs: Chariot Victor, 1999.
- Paul E. Little. *Know Why You Believe.* Revised and updated. Downers Grove, Ill: InterVarsity Press, 2000.
- Erwin W. Lutzer. *Seven Reasons Why You Can Trust the Bible.* Chicago: Moody Press, 1998.

people you respect for their life, their mind, their character, and their faith, and learn from them. Watch their life.

"And I encourage people to put faith-building materials into their minds. By that, I mean books and music that build strong motivation for faith, that give you hope that you can connect with God, that give you tools to develop your own faith."

I like those suggestions. They make sense, but they're not rigid—they can be adapted to *your* needs and *your* life. Applying the principle of going where faith is can be as personal and individual as you are. For help in applying that principle in your own life, use the "Personal Planner" below.

Put Your Faith in the Right Place

"We Canadians know that there are two kinds of ice: thick and thin," Anderson told me. "You can have very little faith in thick ice, and it will hold you up just fine anyway; you can

Personal Planner

People I know **whose faith** I respect:

•

•

"Faith-building materials" (books, music, etc.) I could look into—or someone or someplace I could go to find out about some:

•

•

My personal **"North Poles"**—places/people/media that tend to **freeze my faith:**

•

•

have enormous faith in thin ice—and still fall through and drown. It's not really a question of *how much* faith you have. Your faith may be tiny, like a mustard seed. The question is: Have you invested your faith in something solid?

"That's why people need to know *why* they believe. Why should they believe in Jesus rather than the maharishi? Why do they believe in crystals or in Oriental mysticism? Is that thick ice or thin?" Anderson smiled. "Obviously, I'm prejudiced," he said, "but when it comes right down to it, the only person or thing I know of worth my faith—the only one supported by the evidence of history and archaeology and literature and experience—is Jesus."

That's a big statement to make, and one I didn't always accept. I tell the story of my investigation of the evidence in *The Case for Christ—Student Edition*, so I won't retell it here. If you're wondering whether Jesus is worth your faith, I encourage you to check it out for yourself.

FAITH EXPERIMENT

So how does this faith journey begin?

"Sitting and thinking about faith and doubt will never make a believer out of anyone," was Anderson's response. "Neither will reading the right books or hanging out with the right people or even simply *deciding* to believe. Ultimately, you have to make your own faith experiment by *doing* what faith would do.

"In other words, *do* what Jesus says and you'll experience its validity for yourself. It's kind of like riding a bicycle. You can't learn by watching a video or reading a book about it; you've got to get on one and get the feel of it."

"How does a person do that?" I asked.

"You start by saying to yourself, 'I've heard some things Jesus taught. They sound good, but I don't know if they're true. For instance, I've heard that Jesus said it's more blessed to give than to receive. How can I know if that's true?'

"Well, a thousand debates won't prove it. But when you become generous, you'll realize that Jesus spoke the truth.

"Even after you prove that to yourself, your response might be, 'OK, he was right about that one—but maybe it was just a lucky guess.' Then just keep going. You'll be amazed at how often he 'guessed' right!"

I picked up Anderson's Bible and flipped through it until I came to Psalm 34:8. "King David said, 'Taste and see that the LORD is good,'" I said. "Is that what you're talking about?"

"That's the idea," he agreed. "The more you do this, the more you'll experience what faith is all about."

"Do you ever have moments when you still doubt?" I asked.

"Oh, man, yeah!" he exclaimed. "Even so, these days I'm experiencing God more than ever. I can even see God's grace in those times when he feels far away from me. It's like I'm more aware of what I care about in my best friend when he's gone—and I miss him.

"It's funny—I don't feel like I have all the answers about faith and doubt. But you know what? That doesn't matter to me like it used to. Because I know that what I believe is true. I see it.

"I see it in my life, I see it in my family, I see it in my relationships, I see it in other people's lives when they're changed by the power of God."

Anderson's voice had an undercurrent of confidence. Then, with a ring of finality, he declared, "Lee, I've tried it. I've tasted. And I've seen that the Lord is good!"

The Power of Faith

WHAT NOW?

That's the question I asked myself when I originally investigated the objections to Christianity I've been discussing in this book. Is the problem of suffering, or of hell, a strong enough objection to keep me from accepting Jesus? Do I still think that science contradicts the belief in a Creator capable of doing miracles? Am I willing to make an experiment of faith and choose to believe that Jesus is the only way to God, or do my doubts still get in the way?

You might be asking yourself those same questions. Maybe most of Christianity makes sense to you, but you're hung up on one or two objections. For me, the most troubling were the problems of suffering and hell. For you, it might be something different.

THE BIG PICTURE

Maybe a conversation I had will help you gain some perspective. I'd been talking with my friend

J. P. Moreland about hell. As I was leaving, he said, "Lee, there's something else I need to mention." He seemed frustrated about how to say it. Finally he gave an analogy that created an "Aha!" moment for me.

"When you're trying to make a decision about something, weighing the evidence for and against it, it's important to see the whole picture and not just a little piece of it," he began. "You and I have been focusing on one objection to Christianity—the existence of hell. If you just concentrate on one obstacle, though, you're missing the big picture."

SUSPICIOUS CIRCUMSTANCES

"Let me give you an illustration," J. P. continued. "Suppose I saw my wife embracing another man in a hotel lobby. Would it be reasonable to conclude she was cheating on me?"

I thought that was a question better left unanswered, so I kept quiet.

J. P. went on, "If the only evidence I considered is what I saw at the hotel, then I would probably conclude, 'I don't see anything to show that she's *not* cheating.'"

MORE TO THE STORY

J. P. continued: "But I know my wife well enough to be confident that, while it looks like something funny is going on, it simply *can't* be true that she's cheating. If I'm allowed to bring in a lifetime of evidence about my wife, then it would be clear that there must be another explanation.

"Suppose she'd gotten a phone call from her cousin who lives in Europe—a cousin I've never met, so I wouldn't recognize him. He's in town for a conference, so they agree to meet at the conference hotel to catch up on childhood memories before he goes back to Europe. Now what I saw at the hotel makes perfect sense.

The Case for Faith

"And that's how it is when you're looking into objections to faith. You may be asking yourself, 'Do I buy the concept of hell, or not?' If the only evidence you're considering is the pros and cons of hell itself, that's like looking at my wife's situation and only considering what I saw at the hotel."

WEIGHING THE EVIDENCE

"The problem with that," J. P. said, "is that there's a great deal of evidence that has nothing to do with hell particularly, but it's still relevant. It's all the evidence that there's a God, that he created you, that the New Testament is historically trustworthy, that Jesus performed miracles and rose from the dead, that God wants to spend eternity with you in heaven.

"When you factor all of that in, you might say to yourself, 'Even though I might not have a completely good explanation at this point for why there's a hell (or suffering, or whatever the issue is that gets in your way), I know there's got to *be* an explanation because I have too much evidence that Jesus Christ really is the Son of God, and he taught about these things.

"And because I can trust him and his deep love for people—as demonstrated for us by his death on the cross—I have confidence that hell will eventually make sense, that I'll see its fairness, and I will ultimately recognize it as being the best moral alternative."

He wasn't asking me to take a blind leap of faith by putting my trust in something that didn't make sense and hoping everything will fall into place. He was saying there *is* good evidence that an Intelligent Designer created the universe and fine-tuned it for life and that Jesus *did* prove he's the Son of God by rising from the dead. If that convinces me there must be something to Christianity, then it's logical to take that first step.

Based on the evidence, I could say yes to Jesus and still wrestle with some of my questions over time. In fact, the very process of honestly investigating these issues would bring me closer to God.

That made sense to me. How about you? You may decide, like J. P., that what you know about Jesus outweighs the objections you have. Or you may choose to try to explain away the evidence that points to a Creator. That's the choice I made for much of my life.

ANSWERED PRAYER OR COINCIDENCE?

I'll never forget the day my newborn daughter was rushed into intensive care. A mysterious illness was threatening her life, and the doctors weren't even able to figure out what it was!

Even though I was an atheist at the time, I was so desperate that I actually prayed and begged God—if he existed—to heal her. Several days later, she astounded everyone by suddenly getting completely better. The doctors were left scratching their heads.

My response was to explain it away. I said, "What a coincidence! She must have had some bacteria or virus that suddenly disappeared." I wouldn't even consider the possibility that God had acted.

Even if there had been a hospital chart full of evidence that God had intervened, I would have come up with any explanation—no matter how bizarre or unlikely—other than the possibility that God had answered my prayer. I was too proud to bend the knee to anyone, and too involved in my immoral lifestyle to want to give it up.

BEYOND RIGHT ANSWERS

My mind is capable of manufacturing all kinds of nitpicky arguments and elaborate excuses—even in the face of obvious truth. If I wanted to, I could keep on trying to explain away every sign that God is real and active, including all the evidence for God in this very book. You could too.

Ultimately, though, faith isn't about having perfect and complete answers to every single objection to Christianity. The point is that we do have enough evidence about God on which to act. And in the end, *that's* the issue. Faith is about knowing God personally. It's saying, "I believe—please help me in my unbelief!"

I'm thankful I didn't have to put my brain on hold to become a Christian. The positive evidence for Jesus being the unique Son of God and the convincing answers to my objections cleared the way for me to take that step. But I did have to overcome my pride. I did have to conquer the self-interest and self-centeredness that were keeping my heart shut tight from God.

The biggest issue wasn't whether I had answers to all my questions. The biggest issue was, Did I *want* to know God personally? Did I want to experience release from guilt, to live the way I was designed to live, to pursue his purpose for my life, to tap into his power for daily living, to connect with him in this life and for eternity in the next? If so, there was plenty of evidence on which to base a rational decision to say yes to him.

CHANGING A LIFE

But is there any *point* to saying yes to God? Does it change anything? Does faith really make a difference?

Here's the difference it made to a man named William Moore.

BROTHER MOORE

One Saturday in Atlanta I got into my rental car and took a leisurely drive up Interstate 75 to Rome, Georgia. The next morning was cool but sunny, and I headed over to a church for Sunday services.

Outside, greeting everyone with a handshake as they arrived, was William Neal Moore, looking handsome in a tan suit with dark stripes, a crisp white shirt, and a brown tie. His face was deep mahogany, his black hair cut short, but what I remember most was his smile: it was at once shy and warm, gentle and sincere. It made me feel welcome.

"Praise the Lord, Brother Moore!" declared an elderly woman as she grasped his hand briefly and then shuffled inside.

Moore is an ordained minister at the church, which is sandwiched between two housing projects in the racially mixed community. He is a loving father, a devoted husband, a hardworking employee, a man of compassion and prayer who spends his spare time helping hurting people everyone else seems to have forgotten. In short, a model citizen.

DEATH ROW

But turn back the calendar to May 1984. At that time, Moore was locked in the death-watch cell at the Georgia State Penitentiary, down the hallway from the electric chair where his life was scheduled to be snuffed out in less than 72 hours.

This was not the case of an innocent man being railroaded by the justice system. Unquestionably, Moore was a murderer. He had admitted it. After a childhood of poverty and occasional petty crimes, he had joined the army. After his release, he became depressed over marriage and financial problems. One night he got drunk and broke into the house of 77-year-old Fredger Stapleton, who was known to keep large amounts of cash in his bedroom.

From behind a door, Stapleton let loose with a shotgun blast, and Moore fired back with a pistol. Stapleton was killed instantly, and within minutes Moore was fleeing with $5,600. An informant tipped off the police, and the next morning Moore was arrested at his trailer outside of town. Caught with the money, Moore admitted his guilt and was sentenced to death. He had squandered his life and turned to violence, and now he himself would face a violent end.

A NEW MAN

But the William Neal Moore who was counting down the hours to his scheduled execution was not the same person who had murdered Fredger Stapleton. Shortly after Moore was imprisoned, two church leaders visited him at his mother's request. They told him about the mercy and hope available through Jesus Christ.

"Nobody had ever told me that Jesus loves me and died for me," Moore explained during my visit to Georgia. "It was a love I could feel. It was a love I wanted. It was a love I *needed*."

On that day, Moore said yes to Christ's free gift of forgiveness and eternal life, and he was promptly baptized in a small tub used by prison trustees. He would never be the same.

DEATH ROW MISSIONARY

For 16 years on death row, Moore was like a missionary to the other inmates. He led Bible studies and prayer sessions. He counseled prisoners and introduced many of them to faith in Jesus Christ. Some churches actually sent people to death row to be counseled by him. He took dozens of Bible courses by correspondence. He won the forgiveness of his victim's family. He became known as "The Peacemaker" because his cell block, largely populated by inmates who had become Christians through his influence, was always the safest.

Meanwhile, Moore inched closer and closer to execution. Legally speaking, his case was hopeless. Since he had pleaded guilty, there were virtually no legal issues that might win his release on appeal. Time after time, the courts reaffirmed his death sentence.

Conclusion: The Power of Faith

EXECUTING THE WRONG MAN

Moore's life was so deeply transformed, however, that other people began to take notice. Mother Teresa and others started campaigning to save his life.

"Billy's not what he was then," said a former inmate who had met Moore in prison. "If you kill him today, you're killing a body, but a body with a different mind. It would be like executing the wrong man."

Just hours before Moore was to be strapped into the electric chair, shortly before his head and right calf would be shaved so that the electrodes could be attached, the courts surprised nearly everyone by issuing a temporary halt to his execution.

Even more amazingly, the Georgia Board of Pardons and Parole later voted unanimously to spare his life by changing his sentence to life in prison. But what was *really* astounding—in fact, unheard of in modern Georgia history—was when the Parole and Pardon Board decided that Moore, an admitted and once-condemned armed robber and murderer, should go free. On November 8, 1991, he was released.

THE TRANSFORMATION OF BILLY MOORE

As I sat with Moore in his home overlooking a landscape of lush pines, I asked him about the source of his amazing change. "It was the prison rehabilitation system that did it, right?" I asked.

Moore laughed. "No, it wasn't that."

"Then it was a self-help program or having a positive mental attitude," I suggested.

He shook his head emphatically. "No, not that, either."

"Prozac? Transcendental meditation? Psychological counseling?"

"Come on, Lee," he said. "You know it wasn't any of those."

He was right. I knew the real reason. I just wanted to hear him say it. "Then what was responsible for the transformation of Billy Moore?" I asked.

"Plain and simple, it was Jesus Christ," he declared. "He changed me in ways I could never have changed on my own. He gave me a reason to live. He helped me do the right thing. He gave me a heart for others. He saved my soul."

THE POWER OF FAITH

That's the power of faith to change a human life. "Therefore," wrote the apostle Paul in 2 Corinthians 5:17, "if anyone is in Christ, he is a new creation; the old has gone, the new has come!"

Billy Moore the Christian is not the same as Billy Moore the killer. God intervened with his forgiveness, with his mercy, with his power, and with the presence of his Spirit. That same kind of transforming grace is available to everyone who acts on the evidence for Jesus Christ by making the decision to turn away from their sin and embrace him as their forgiver and leader.

It's there for all those who say yes to God.

Now—it's your call.

CHALLENGE #1

Scholars Are Uncovering a Radically Different Jesus through Ancient Documents Just as Credible as the Four Gospels

The rumor mill was churning. One of my reporters received a tip that police had detained a man running for Illinois governor. The accusation? He'd allegedly abused his wife. If this were true, then the irony would be devastating: One of his responsibilities as the state's chief executive would be to oversee a network of shelters for battered women.

If this politician really had abused his wife, then the voters deserved to know. But before we could responsibly break the story, we needed indisputable confirmation—preferably, a written document—to establish the facts. It would be terrible journalism—not to mention despicable human behavior—to label him an abuser without solid evidence to back up that claim.

The reporters milked their sources. One came up with a timeframe for the incident. Another got the name of the Chicago suburb where the incident allegedly took place in a public parking lot. Still, we didn't have enough. The information was too vague and too unreliable.

Finally, another reporter was able to obtain the key piece of evidence: a police report that described exactly what happened. Because no criminal charges had been filed, privacy laws dictated that all names on the report be blacked out. As the reporter studied the report more carefully, though, she discovered the police had failed to black out the name in one place. Sure enough, it was the candidate's name. Digging deeper in the report yielded the final clue: The suspect had bragged about being the mayor of a certain suburb—the same position held by the candidate. *Bingo!* A match.

In a dramatic confrontation in the *Tribune's* conference room, I peppered the candidate with questions about the incident. He steadfastly denied it ever occurred—until I handed him a copy of the police report. Now faced with the indisputable evidence, he finally admitted to the encounter with police. And within 72 hours, he'd withdrawn from the governor's race.[5]

For both journalists and historians, documents can be invaluable in helping confirm what's happened. Even so, detective work still needs to be done in order to establish the authenticity and credibility of any written record. Questions need to be asked: Who wrote it? Was this person in a position to know what happened? Was he or she motivated by prejudice or bias? Has the document been kept safe from tampering? How legible is it? Is it backed by other external facts? And are there competing documents that might be more reliable or that might shed a whole new light on the matter?

When it comes to understanding the historical Jesus, that last question has become particularly important. For centuries scholars investigating what happened in the life of Jesus relied mostly on the New Testament, especially the books of Mark, Matthew, and Luke—which are the oldest of the four books we call "the Gospels"—as well as the Gospel of John.

In modern times, however, archaeological discoveries have yielded a fascinating crop of other documents from ancient Palestine.

A DIFFERENT JESUS

In the years since my initial investigation into Jesus, the focus on what some scholars call "alternative gospels" has greatly intensified. Both academic and popular books have used these sources to offer a different picture of Jesus. In the 1990s, several participants in the Jesus Seminar (a group of highly liberal and skeptical academics) and others, led by religious studies professor Robert J. Miller, published *The Complete Gospels*, which put the New Testament Gospels side-by-side with 16 other ancient texts.[6]

"Each of these gospel records offers fresh glimpses into the world of Jesus and his followers," says the book.[7] "All of the... texts in this volume are witnesses to early Jesus traditions. All of them contain traditions independent of the New Testament gospels."[8]

THE JESUS SEMINAR

The left-wing Jesus Seminar captivated the media's attention in the 1990s by using colored beads to vote on what Jesus really said. The group's conclusion: Fewer than one in five sayings attributed to Jesus in the Gospels actually came from him. In the Lord's Prayer, the Seminar determined that Jesus said only the words "Our Father." There were similar results when the participants considered which deeds of Jesus were authentic.

What made the Jesus Seminar unique was the way it bypassed the usual academic channels and enthusiastically took its conclusions directly to the public, which was ill-equipped to evaluate them. "These scholars have suddenly become concerned—to the point of being almost evangelistic—with shaping public opinion about Jesus with their research," said one New Testament expert.[9]

A major reason to take these alternative gospels seriously is that some scholars claim they were written as early as the first century, which is when Jesus' ministry flourished and the four Gospels of the New Testament were written. If that's the case, then we can assume they contain very early—and perhaps historically reliable—material.

To me, the implication of this research was clear: These other gospels—with such names as the Gospel of Thomas, the Secret Gospel of Mark, the Gospel of Peter, and the Gospel of Mary—were equal to the biblical accounts in terms of their historical significance and spiritual content. In fact, Philip Jenkins, professor of history and religious studies at Pennsylvania State University, said, "With so many hidden gospels now brought to light, it is now often claimed that the four Gospels were simply four among many of roughly equal worth, and the alternative texts gave just as valid a picture of Jesus as the texts we have today."[10]

The discovery of these other gospels might not be such a big deal if they gave pretty much the same picture of Jesus that the New Testament gives. But some of them paint a very different portrait of Jesus from the one we find in the Bible, and they throw key theological beliefs into question. To see what I mean, Google "Gospel of Thomas." You can find the entire book—a collection of 114 sayings that are attributed to Jesus—online. What you'll read will have some similarities to the New Testament Gospels, but you'll also find some significant differences. Here are a few examples:

SUBJECT	GOSPEL OF THOMAS	NEW TESTAMENT
Who Jesus is	Someone who imparts secret teachings to the disciples who are mature enough to receive it	The Redeemer who saves his people from sin
Salvation	Salvation comes through a special, secret knowledge. You have to be worthy to receive that knowledge.	Salvation comes through faith in Jesus. "And you can't take credit for this; it is a gift from God" (Ephesians 2:8, NLT).
Fasting, prayer, and giving	"If you fast, you will bring sin upon yourselves, and if you pray, you will be condemned, and if you give to charity, you will harm your spirits." (Saying 14)	"When you fast, comb your hair and wash your face" (Matthew 6:17, NLT). "And pray in the Spirit on all occasions with all kinds of prayers and requests" (Ephesians 6:18). "If [your gift] is contributing to the needs of others... give generously" (Romans 12:8).

And that's only one small sampling of one document. Take a look at some of the other alternative gospels:

- The Gospel of Mary: Contrary to the biblical Gospels, this text has Jesus teaching that "salvation is achieved by seeking the true spiritual nature of humanity within oneself and overcoming the entrapping material nature of the body and the world."[11]

- The Secret Gospel of Mark: The most controversial claim in this gospel is that Jesus conducted a secret initiation rite with a young man that, according to one scholar, may have included "physical union."[12]

- The Jesus Papers: Directly contradicting what Christianity has taught for two millennia, Jesus explicitly denies that he's the Son of God, clarifying instead that he only embodies God's spirit as anyone can.[13]

- The Gospel of Judas: The most sensational claims in this text are that Judas Iscariot was Jesus' greatest disciple, that he alone was able to understand Jesus' most profound teaching, and that the two of them conspired to arrange for Jesus' betrayal.

All of this had profound implications for my personal quest to discover the real Jesus. Was it possible my earlier conclusions about him had been unduly colored by New Testament accounts that were really only one perspective among many?

Clearly, a lot was at stake. I needed to have confidence that the *right* people used the *right* reasoning to choose the *right* documents in the ancient world. I needed to know if there was any historical support for these alternative texts that cast Jesus in a different light. I needed to go wherever the evidence took me.

Knowing there are almost as many opinions as there are experts, I wanted to track down someone with sterling credentials, who would be respected by both conservatives *and* liberals, and who, most importantly, could back up any insights with solid facts and reasoning.

That meant flying to Nova Scotia and driving to a quaint village to interview a highly regarded historian. After driving more than an hour from my hotel in Halifax, I ended up in a heavily wooded community near Acadia University. I rang the doorbell at the colonial-style home of Craig A. Evans, professor of New Testament at Acadia.

I believed Evans could help me determine whether these alternative gospels are trustworthy and give me some insight into the way Bible scholars sort out the fact from the fiction.

The Case for the Real Jesus – Student Edition

A Journalist Investigates Current Challenges to Christianity

Lee Strobel with Jane Vogel

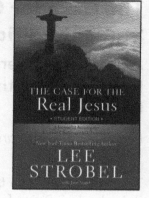

Just about everyone you ask has an opinion about Jesus. Some believe he was the Son of God, while others question his existence altogether. Some believe he lived, but that he was merely a good man. Today, scientists and other people are making statements that can make it difficult to know what to believe. So how can you know who the real Jesus was (and is)—especially when so many people are working to prove him to be a fake or a fraud? That's what Lee Strobel wanted to know.

As a former journalist—and a former atheist—Lee went on an investigative journey to discover the real Jesus, one that took him across the continent and

into the homes of today's most prominent experts on Christian history. He found all the evidence he needed to believe that the Jesus is indeed the Risen Savior.

Join Lee's investigation and discover the truth about Jesus for yourself. After you've seen all the evidence, you'll know for certain who the real Jesus is, and you'll be able to help others know him as well.

Available in stores and online!

The Case for Christ — Student Edition

A Journalist's Personal Investigation of the Evidence for Jesus

Lee Strobel with Jane Vogel

There's little question that he actually lived. But miracles? Rising from the dead? Some of the stories you hear about him sound like just that — stories. A reasonable person would never believe them, let alone the claim that he's the only way to God!

But a reasonable person would also make sure that he or she understood the facts before jumping to conclusions. That's why Lee Strobel — an award-winning legal journalist with a knack for asking tough questions — decided to investigate Jesus for himself. An atheist, Strobel felt certain his findings would bring Christianity's claims about Jesus tumbling down like a house of cards.

He was in for the surprise of his life. Join him as he retraces his journey from skepticism to faith. You'll consult expert testimony as you sift through the truths that history, science, psychiatry, literature, and religion reveal. Like Strobel, you'll be amazed at the evidence — how much there is, how strong it is, and what it says.

The facts are in. What will your verdict be in *The Case for Christ*?

The Case for a Creator - Student Edition

A Journalist Investigates Scientific Evidence That Points Toward God

Lee Strobel with Jane Vogel

In *The Case for a Creator—Student Edition*, best-selling author and former atheist Lee Strobel and popular writer Jane Vogel take younger readers on a remarkable investigation into the origin of the universe, interviewing many of the world's most renown scientists and following the evidence wherever it leads.

Their findings—presented in the third blockbuster "Case" book student edition—offer the most compelling scientific proof ever for intelligent design. Perfect for youth groups and young people eager to rebut the Darwinian and naturalistic views taught so commonly in schools.

Available in stores and online!

The Case for Faith

A Journalist Investigates the Toughest Objections to Christianity

Lee Strobel
New York Times *Bestselling Author*

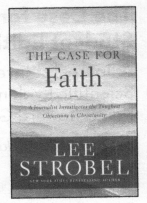

Was God telling the truth when he said, "You will seek me and find me when you seek me with all your heart"?

In his #1 bestseller *The Case for Christ*, Lee Strobel examined the claims of Christ, reaching the hard-won verdict that Jesus is God's unique son. In *The Case for Faith*, Strobel turns his skills to the most persistent emotional objections to belief—the eight "heart barriers" to faith. This Gold Medallion-winning book is for those who may be feeling attracted to Jesus but who are faced with difficult questions standing squarely in their path. For Christians, it will deepen their convictions and give them fresh confidence in discussing Christianity with even their most skeptical friends.

> *"Everyone—seekers, doubters, fervent believers—benefits when Lee Strobel hits the road in search of answers, as he does again in The Case for Faith. In the course of his probing interviews, some of the toughest intellectual obstacles to faith fall away."*
>
> Luis Palau

> *"Lee Strobel has given believers and skeptics alike a gift in this book. He does not avoid seeking the most difficult questions imaginable, and refuses to provide simplistic answers that do more harm than good."*
>
> **Jerry Sittser**, professor of religion, Whitworth College, and author of *A Grace Disguised* and *The Will of God as a Way of Life*

Available in stores and online!

The Case for Christ

A Journalist's Personal Investigation of the Evidence for Jesus

Lee Strobel
New York Times *Bestselling Author*

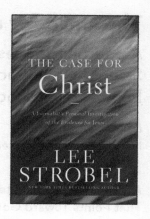

A Seasoned Journalist Chases Down the Biggest Story in History

Is there credible evidence that Jesus of Nazareth really is the Son of God?

Retracing his own spiritual journey from atheism to faith, Lee Strobel, former legal editor of the *Chicago Tribune*, cross-examines a dozen experts with doctorates from schools like Cambridge, Princeton, and Brandeis who are recognized authorities in their own fields.

Strobel challenges them with questions like How reliable is the New Testament? Does evidence for Jesus exist outside the Bible? Is there any reason to believe the resurrection was an actual event?

Strobel's tough, point-blank questions make this Gold Medallion-winning book read like a captivating, fast-paced novel. But it's not fiction. It's a riveting quest for the truth about history's most compelling figure.

What will your verdict be in *The Case for Christ*?

"Lee Strobel probes with bulldog-like tenacity the evidence for the truth of biblical Christianity."

Bruce M. Metzger, PhD, Professor of New Testament, Emeritus, Princeton Theological Seminary

"Lee Strobel asks the questions a tough-minded skeptic would ask. His book is so good I read it out loud to my wife evenings after dinner. Every inquirer should have it."

Phillip E. Johnson, Law Professor, University of California at Berkeley

Available in stores and online!

ZONDERVAN®
.com

The Case for a Creator

A Journalist Investigates Scientific Evidence That Points Toward God

Lee Strobel
New York Times *Bestselling Author*

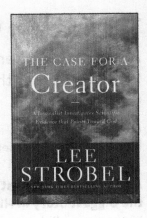

A Journalist Investigates Scientific Evidence
That Points Toward God

> *"My road to atheism was paved by science . . . But, ironically, so was my later journey to God."* — **Lee Strobel**

During his academic years, Lee Strobel became convinced that God was outmoded, a belief that colored his ensuing career as an award-winning journalist at the *Chicago Tribune*. Science had made the idea of a Creator irrelevant — or so Strobel thought.

But today science is pointing in a different direction. In recent years, a diverse and impressive body of research has increasingly supported the conclusion that the universe was intelligently designed. At the same time, Darwinism has faltered in the face of concrete facts and hard reason.

Has science discovered God? At the very least, it's giving faith an immense boost as new findings emerge about the incredible complexity of our universe. Join Strobel as he reexamines the theories that once led him away from God. Through his compelling and highly readable account, you'll encounter the mind-stretching discoveries from cosmology, cellular biology, DNA research, astronomy, physics, and human consciousness that present astonishing evidence in *The Case for a Creator*.

Available in stores and online!

The Case for the Real Jesus

A Journalist Investigates Current Attacks on the Identity of Christ

Lee Strobel
New York Times *Bestselling Author*

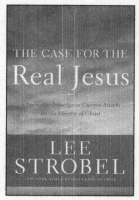

Has modern scholarship debunked the traditional Christ? Has the church suppressed the truth about Jesus to advance its own agenda? What if the real Jesus is far different from the atoning Savior worshipped through the centuries?

In *The Case for the Real Jesus*, former award-winning legal editor Lee Strobel explores such hot-button questions as:

- Did the church suppress ancient non-biblical documents that paint a more accurate picture of Jesus than the four Gospels?
- Did the church distort the truth about Jesus by tampering with early New Testament texts?
- Do new insights and explanations finally disprove the resurrection?
- Have fresh arguments disqualified Jesus from being the Messiah?
- Did Christianity steal its core ideas from earlier mythology?

Evaluate the arguments and evidence being advanced by prominent atheists, liberal theologians, Muslim scholars, and others. Sift through expert testimony. Then reach your own verdict in *The Case for the Real Jesus*.

Available in stores and online!

ZONDERVAN®
.com

Talk It Up!

Want free books?
First looks at the best new fiction?
Awesome exclusive merchandise?

We want to hear from you!

Give us your opinions on titles, covers, and stories.
Join the Z Street Team.

Visit zstreetteam.zondervan.com/joinnow
to sign up today!

Also—Friend us on Facebook!

www.facebook.com/goodteenreads

- Video Trailers
- Connect with your favorite authors
- Sneak peeks at new releases
- Giveaways
- Fun discussions
- And much more!